*Another Look At
The Ten Commandments*

The Big Ten

Ron Lavin

CSS Publishing Company, Inc., Lima, Ohio

THE BIG TEN

Copyright © 2005 by
CSS Publishing Company, Inc.
Lima, Ohio

All rights reserved. No part of this publication may be reproduced in any manner whatsoever without the prior permission of the publisher, except in the case of brief quotations embodied in critical articles and reviews. Inquiries should be addressed to: Permissions, CSS Publishing Company, Inc., P.O. Box 4503, Lima, Ohio 45802-4503.

Unless otherwise marked, scripture quotations are taken from the *Holy Bible, New International Version*. Copyright © 1973, 1978, 1984 International Bible Society. Used by permission of Zondervan Bible Publishers. All rights reserved.

Scripture quotations marked (NRSV) are from the *New Revised Standard Version of the Bible*, copyright 1989 by the Division of Christian Education of the National Council of the Churches of Christ in the USA. Used by permission.

Scripture quotations marked (RSV) are from the *Revised Standard Version of the Bible*, copyrighted 1946, 1952 ©, 1971, 1973, by the Division of Christian Education of the National Council of the Churches of Christ in the USA. Used by permission.

Library of Congress Cataloging-in-Publication Data

Lavin, Ronald J.
  The big ten : another look at the Ten commandments / Ron Lavin.
    p. cm.
  Includes bibliographical references.
  ISBN 0-7880-2348-9 (alk. paper)
  1. Ten commandments. 2., Christian life—Lutheran authors. I. Title.

BV4655.L29 2005
241.5'2—dc22

200402990

For more information about CSS Publishing Company resources, visit our website at www.csspub.com or e-mail us at custserv@csspub.com or call (800) 241-4056.

ISBN 0-7880-2348-9   PRINTED IN U.S.A.

*This book is dedicated to
our eight grandchildren
in the hope that the faith will be passed on
to generations yet to come.*

*Lydia Wilkinson
Sarah Wilkinson
Heidi Wilkinson
David Pflibsen
Peter Pflibsen
Jimmy Cousler
Stephen Cousler
and
Tommy Cousler*

He (God) decreed statutes for Jacob and established the law in Israel, which he commanded our forefathers to teach their children so the next generation would know them, even the children yet to be born, and they in turn would tell their children. They would put their trust in God and would not forget his deeds but would keep his commands.
— Psalm 78:5-7

Books By Ron Lavin

The *Another Look* Series
I Believe; Help My Unbelief: Another Look At The Apostles' Creed
Stories To Remember: Another Look At The Parables Of Jesus
Abba: Another Look At The Lord's Prayer
Saving Grace: Another Look At The Word And The Sacraments
The Big Ten: Another Look At The Ten Commandments

Coming Soon:
People Who Met Jesus: Another Look At The Suffering, Death, And Resurrection Of Our Lord

Other Books In Print
Turning Griping Into Gratitude
Empty Spaces; Empty Places (written with Constance Sorenson)
Way To Grow! (Dynamic Church Growth Through Small Groups)
The Advocate
The Great I AM
Previews Of Coming Attractions

Previously Published Books
Alone / Together
You Can't Start A Car With A Cross
Roots And Wings
You Can Grow In A Small Group
Small Groups Can Change Your Church
The Human Chain For Divine Grace (editor)
Jesus In Stained Glass
Jesus Christ, The Liberator (written with Bill Grimmer, M.D.)
Hey, Mom, Look At Me!

And God spoke all these words:
"I am the LORD your God, who brought you out of Egypt, out of the land of slavery.
"You shall have no other gods before me.
"You shall not make for yourself an idol in the form of anything in heaven above or on the earth beneath or in the waters below ...
"You shall not misuse the name of the LORD your God, for the LORD will not hold anyone guiltless who misuses his name.
"Remember the Sabbath day by keeping it holy ...
"Honor your father and your mother, so that you may live long in the land the LORD your God is giving you.
"You shall not murder.
"You shall not commit adultery.
"You shall not steal.
"You shall not give false testimony against your neighbor.
"You shall not covet your neighbor's house.
"You shall not covet your neighbor's wife, or his manservant or maidservant, his ox or donkey, or anything that belongs to your neighbor."
— Exodus 20:1-17

Praise the LORD!
Happy are those who
fear the LORD,
who greatly delight in
his commandments.
— Psalm 112:1 (NRSV)

On one occasion an expert in the law stood up to test Jesus. "Teacher," he asked, "what must I do to inherit eternal life?"

"What is written in the Law?" he [Jesus] replied. "How do you read it?"

He answered: " 'Love the Lord your God with all you heart and with all your soul and with all your strength and with all your mind' and 'Love your neighbor as yourself.' "

"You have answered correctly," Jesus replied. "Do this and you will live."

— Luke 10:25-28

Table Of Contents

A Personal Word About The *Another Look* Series   9

Introduction   11
  By Dr. Mel Kieschnick

Prologue   13

Foundations
Foundations   21

The Ten Commandments
The First Table Of The Law
1. Prohibitions And Invitations In The
   First Commandment   31
2. Prohibitions And Invitations In The
   Second Commandment   39
3. Prohibitions And Invitations In The
   Third Commandment   49

The Second Table Of The Law
4. Prohibitions And Invitations In The
   Fourth Commandment   61
5. Prohibitions And Invitations In The
   Fifth Commandment   73
6. Prohibitions And Invitations In The
   Sixth Commandment   85
7. Prohibitions And Invitations In The
   Seventh Commandment   97
8. Prohibitions And Invitations In The
   Eighth Commandment   107
9. Prohibitions And Invitations In The
   Ninth Commandment   117
10. Prohibitions And Invitations In The
    Tenth Commandment   125

The Eleventh Commandment
11. Prohibitions And Invitations In The
    Eleventh Commandment   139

12. Life Begins At Forty   149

Seven Tips For Leaders   153

Endnotes   155

A Personal Word About The *Another Look* Series

The Big Ten, is the fifth book in the *Another Look* series. The topic in this book is the Ten Commandments. The first book in the series is *I Believe: Help My Unbelief* (on the Apostles' Creed). The second is *Stories To Remember* (on the parables of Jesus). The third is *Abba* (on the Lord's Prayer). The fourth is *Saving Grace* (on the sacraments). All are available from CSS Publishing Company, Lima, Ohio.

The Big Ten and the other books in the series are ideal for membership instruction classes. These books may be used as supplementary materials for new members. As pastors instruct new members, there is no way to cover the rich heritage of the history and essentials of our faith. These books provide a helpful overview of the Christian faith. Many people today are hungry for knowledge, especially in the area of religion. This series will help seekers get in touch with our Christian heritage.

Confirmation teachers and confirmation classes will find this material useful. Adult classes on Sunday or weekdays will find this series useful. It is hard to find good materials for these classes. Bible study groups and other small groups that meet in homes and churches will find the *Another Look* series the answer to their search.

There are two major movements in American churches today. One is lay ministry development. The second is the small group movement. Small groups need study materials for lay ministry development. The books in this series provide excellent topics for small group discussion and lay ministry development.

When it comes to small group ministry and lay ministry development, I am a believer. I have started over 500 small groups and written three books on small groups and lay ministry development. They are:
- *Way To Grow!*
- *You Can Grow In A Small Group*
- *A Strategy For Renewal*

At conferences where I have spoken and in the five churches I have served, small groups have been used as a key strategy to bring people together and deepen their faith. These groups worked well in small churches and large ones. The size of the five churches I have served varied from a mission church in Lebanon, Indiana, that served only fifteen people when I arrived, to a congregation of about 5,000 members in Davenport, Iowa. All of these churches grew significantly in spirituality, membership, and worship attendance. Small groups are not a panacea for what is wrong with our churches, but they are an integral part of spiritual and numerical church growth.

Questions at the end of each chapter and the section called Digging Deeper in the books in this series make them ideal tools for all kinds of study groups. The books offer solid study material for retreats. They can also be given to doubters, seekers, agnostics, and atheists who are often outside the church because they don't understand the Christian faith. When unbelievers say they don't believe in God, you can ask them to tell you about the god they don't believe in. Often the god they don't believe in is not the God and Father of our Lord Jesus Christ. Give these books to unbelievers and help free them from their illusions about the one true God.

The books in this series not only help us go back to the basics; they help us go forward with the basics. Without the basics of our faith in place, how can we advance?

Introduction

By Dr. Mel Kieschnick
Former Executive Director of Education,
Lutheran Church — Missouri Synod
Former Assistant to the Bishop, New York Synod, ELCA

The Ten Commandments are both in and out of the news these days. They are in the news because there are significant voices calling for them to be posted in classrooms and courtrooms. When our nation faces the challenge of internal moral decline or external terrorist attacks some people look to the Ten Commandments to point the way to national security. How effective (or constitutional) this suggested remedy might be remains open to lively debate.

On the other hand, there are voices saying the Ten Commandments are irrelevant in today's world. With the denial of the existence of any absolute truth or moral standards, the Ten Commandments seem to be little more than an artifact of an ancient patriarchal society. In a culture that emphasizes personal choice based almost exclusively on personal values and needs, God-given structures sometimes seem too restrictive.

The Big Ten takes another view. It presents challenges and invitations to take another look at the Ten Commandments. It posits that the Ten Commandments continue to provide both significant prohibitions and helpful invitations for living a moral and godly life in the twenty-first century.

This book serves as a helpful resource for both private reflection and group interaction. The author and I taught this series in an adult class of our congregation at Calvary Lutheran Church in Solana Beach, California. When we stimulated discussion and mined the wisdom of the group, thought-provoking new insights were shared. We looked at the First Commandment while in Afghanistan artillery shells were blasting away centuries-old Buddhas sculpted into the mountain. How does this relate to the First Commandment?

While we studied the Fifth Commandment, the U.S. Supreme Court ruled unconstitutional the Oregon statute permitting (under very limited conditions) doctors to prescribe fatal dosages of drugs to one considered terminally ill. During the same class we explored whether the World Trade terrorists were murderers while those who dropped bombs on Afghanistan were not. The whole issue of pacifism and the just-war theory surfaced for lively discussion.

One final example: spirited discussion on the Ninth and Tenth Commandments dealt with the theory that "Covetousness has helped make America great." What a discussion!

For each of the sessions this book provided not only the author's insight, but also references to biblical sources that needed to be heard. The Digging Deeper section at the end of each chapter proved to be particularly helpful. Our class became a community of moral deliberation as we studied *The Big Ten*.

Further, the class kept asking of each Commandment, "What is it that God is protecting here?" It was refreshing to deal with a resource that pointed not only to prohibitions but also to invitations.

I found this book a good resource for personal reading and reflection as well as an excellent tool for group study. I did not post the Ten Commandments on my classroom wall, but they were imprinted more boldly onto my heart. May you have a similar experience.

Prologue

"Why write a book called *The Big Ten*?" a friend asked. "Because on a scale of one to ten, ten is the highest you can go," I replied. When we say that a person is a ten, we mean that they are exceptional. When we say that a program is a ten, we mean that it is excellent. *The Big Ten*, the title of this book on the Ten Commandments, is intended to convey that God's Law is not only exceptional, but excellent in every way. The Commandments are God's Big Ten.

What are the presenting problems that make me believe that this topic is relevant today? Many people are adrift spiritually. People are creating their own religions to fill the void. Religions that people create never fill the hole in their souls. We need to look again at the Ten Commandments to get us back on the track that leads to hope and eternal life.

Why are the Ten Commandments so important for today? Let me cite three reasons. First, the Commandments help us to identify our sins. Without this identification, we do not repent. Without repentance, we will not be forgiven. Without forgiveness, life is hopeless. Christ is the answer to peoples' hopelessness, but the question has to be raised before the answer is understood. The Ten Commandments raise questions about our sinful condition, for which the answer is the Savior. The itch has to be identified before we move to the scratch.

Second, we live in a time when many people are caught in the web of ethical relativism. Ethical relativism teaches that there are no absolutes. Great biblical truths, like the Ten Commandments, have guided generation after generation before us. Today many people toss these Commandments to the sidelines as mere human opinions. When great moral principles are discarded as if they were no more than personal opinions, catastrophes follow. In San Diego, California, where I live, two shootings in public high schools and another shooting in a low income nursing home resulted in the deaths of young and old alike. Our nation experienced major tragedy on September 11, 2001, when terrorists paid no attention to the Law of God about murder.

Do these tragedies have anything to do with the fact that illusions of God have replaced the biblical picture of God and the high teachings God's Big Ten? Isn't the philosophy of "Me-First, Last, And Always" bound to fail because it is the direct opposite of the teaching of the Bible? Isn't there a connection between what is happening in our society and the ethical relativism being taught in our schools and embraced by many today? Yes! Yes! Yes!

God is absolute. His Law is absolute. The Ten Commandments are not just the personal opinions of ancient Jews and Christians. They are not the Ten Suggestions, but the sovereign Commandments of the sovereign God. People who break the Commandments and see no need for repentance are broken by them.

We need to repent for sins that have been committed. In order to repent, we need to have sins identified. In order to come to faith in Jesus as our Savior we need to face our sins honestly. We need the Ten Commandments to do that. We also need the Ten Commandments to overcome the challenge of ethical relativism that teaches that there are no absolutes.

Third, there are some people who believe that while there are laws against certain kinds of immoral behavior for others, they see themselves as exceptions to these laws. This is a major problem in our time.

In Fyodor Dostoevsky's *Crime And Punishment*, the leading character, Roskolnikov, insists that he is above the law. He buries a hatchet in the head of an old pawn-broker. He says that he doesn't feel guilty for his action because the law does not apply to him. The law may apply to others, but, he says, he is above the morality of the crowd. This classic novel is all about the consequences of the sin of suspending, or more accurately, trying to suspend, the laws of God. Acting as if you are above the laws of God always results in catastrophe for individuals and society.

In *The Brothers Karamazov*, Dostoevsky makes this astute observation: "Where there is no God, all is permitted." Are we really living in a time when most people have no God? In spite of the fact that the vast majority of Americans claim that they believe in

God, on closer examination, we see that we live in a nation where most people are practical atheists. Many people say that they believe in God, but they live as if there is no God. Practical atheists may want God to comfort them in times of stress and troubles, but they do not want to live under God's authority. God as a parachute — useless except in emergencies — is no God at all. That is why we must get back to the basics of the Ten Commandments. We don't just need to get back to God's Law. We must love God's Law and do our best to follow the Law. When we fail, we must come to true repentance before God in order to go forward.

The gospel of salvation through Jesus Christ lifts us out of our sins, but we cannot have the gospel without recognition of sin. As Dietrich Bonhoeffer put it, "There is a cost of discipleship." Jesus paid the price for our sins, but if we insist on cheap grace — grace without commitment — we not only miss out on grace, we get caught in the chaos of the world. Chaos is catching. We too easily succumb. Salvation is free, but it is not cheap.

Salvation has been accomplished for everyone, but not everyone receives the benefits of what Christ did for them on the cross. Christ's work of redemption is like God giving us a check for a million dollars. We can stick the check in the drawer and never use it. We can light up a cigar with it. Or we can turn the check over, endorse it, and receive the benefits of the gift. We endorse what Jesus has done for us on the cross by acknowledging that we are sinful and do not deserve the gift. When we personally sign the check, we discover a surprise called the abundant life.

The aim of each chapter in this book is to help us see not only God's prohibitions, but his invitations to the abundant life. The wonders of life in abundance for the believer are discovered as we rediscover the Father's love behind each of his prohibitions.

The intended use of this book is for personal inspiration and for groups and classes in our churches. Confirmation classes, adult instruction classes, Sunday school classes for adults and teenagers, and small groups meeting in the homes will all benefit from the study of *The Big Ten*. *The Big Ten* can also be used on retreats. Study guides with questions for discussion are provided at the end of each chapter for further consideration of the questions raised in the chapters. A section at the end of each chapter called Digging Deeper is a call to extended and deeper consideration.

At this point, you may want to turn to Seven Tips For Leaders at the back of this book. This section will give you ideas about how this book may be used.

The dedication of this book is to my eight grandchildren "so the next generation (and following generations) will know the statutes of God" (Psalm 78:6). If today is a difficult time to stick to the ways of the Lord, how much more difficult will it be when our children's children have children of their own?

The section of this book I call Foundations is intended to lay down in a straightforward way the Old and New Testament basis for what follows in this book. Hopefully, it will whet your appetite and make you want to read more.

The people to whom I am grateful for their teachings on the basics of the faith include not only theologians like George Forell, Pat Keifert, and my seminary professors, but family members who have lived out the faith and called me to do the same. I can never express enough gratitude to the many lay men and women who have served as leaders in the five churches I have served in the past 44 years of ministry. In addition, I am grateful to Tom Lentz, Terry Rhodes, Rebecca Brandt, and Stan Purdum, my editors at CSS Publishing Company, who have been outstanding as publication partners for this book and fifteen others.

Calvary Lutheran Church in Selona Beach, California, has been the place where all of the materials in the books in the *Another Look* series have been field-tested before final publication. Other churches where these materials have been tested include San Marcos Lutheran Church in San Marcos, California; King of Glory Lutheran Church in Fountain Valley, California; Shepherd of the Hills Lutheran Church in Alpine, California; Our Saviour's Lutheran Church in Tucson, Arizona; St. Paul Lutheran Church in Davenport, Iowa; Holy Trinity Lutheran Church in Muncie, Indiana; and Trinity Lutheran Church in Lebanon, Indiana. My thanks to the leaders and participants in these churches for helping to refine my ideas with their comments and suggestions.

Special thanks to Mel Kieschnick, who wrote the Introduction to this book. Mel and I co-teach many adult classes at Calvary Lutheran Church in Encinitas, California. He has written the Introduction for two of my previous books in the *Another Look* series. Mel, and his wife Jane, are special friends and advisors.

The order of the Ten Commandments used in this book is the one used by Lutherans and Roman Catholics with two commandments on coveting. Most Protestants and Jews use the order with two commandments on idolatry. Unfortunately, when Moses got the Commandments from God, there were no numbers attached to them.

> Ron Lavin
> phone for speaking engagements
> (760) 634-7734

Foundations

Foundations

Moses summoned all Israel and said: Hear O Israel, the decrees and laws I declare in your hearing today. Learn them and follow them. — Deuteronomy 5:1

Hear, O Israel: The LORD our God, the LORD is one. Love the LORD your God with all of your heart and with all of your soul and with all your strength. These commandments that I give you today are to be upon your hearts. Impress them on your children. Talk about them when you sit at home and when you walk along the road, when you lie down and when you get up. Tie them as symbols on your hands and bind them on your foreheads. Write them on the doorframes of your houses and on your gates. — Deuteronomy 6:4-9

[Jesus said] "Do not think that I have come to abolish the Law or the Prophets; I have not come to abolish them but to fulfill them. I tell you the truth, until heaven and earth disappear, not the smallest letter, not the least stroke of a pen, will by any means disappear from the Law until everything is accomplished."
— Matthew 5:17-18

An expert on the Jewish Law once tried to challenge Jesus and trick him. He asked a question: "What must I do to inherit eternal life?"

Jesus answered his question with a question: "What is written in the Law?"

The lawyer answered: "Love the Lord your God with all your heart and with all your soul and with all your strength and with all your mind, and love your neighbor as yourself."
Jesus told him that this is the correct answer but added, "Do this and you will live" (Luke 10:25-28).
The law of loving God and neighbors is the summary of the Ten Commandments. The two invitations in this summary are reverence for God and respect for our neighbors. The first three commandments about idolatry, God's name, and God's Sabbath day, are called the first table of the Law. The last seven commandments deal with our relationships with one another. We are called to respect other people's lives and property. Loving the Lord God and loving our neighbors as we love ourselves are the foundation of life. Knowing this summary of the Ten Commandments is not enough; we must practice what we know.

The command to love God and our neighbors is not a foundation for our lives just because we can repeat this formula. The command to love the Lord and neighbors as we love ourselves must be put into action if it is to be the real foundation of our lives.

These words from the Old and New Testaments are not only the foundation of Judaism and Christianity. These words are the foundation of life. The Lord God is not one God among many; not the best God of a variety of gods, but the one and only God. All other gods are false gods. That's what the Bible means by saying "the Lord is one."

In one sense, these words about loving God and following his Law are commands. The Ten Commandments are not the Ten Suggestions. They are commands from the Lord, the absolute authority for our lives. There are serious consequences to not obeying these commands. The Ten Commandments are prohibitions.

In another sense, these words are invitations. If you follow these invitations to love the Lord your God, and your neighbors, your life will be integrated, full, and whole. To the extent that you do not follow these invitations, your life will be disintegrated, divided, and fragmented. That is what we mean by saying that the call to love the Lord and your neighbor is foundational. You can only build a meaningful life if you embrace the love of the Lord and pass that love on to your neighbors.

You cannot build a house that will last unless you build on a firm foundation. Jesus put it this way:

> ... *Everyone who hears these words of mine and puts them into practice is like a wise man who built his house on the rock. The rain came down, the streams rose, and the winds blew and beat against that house; yet it did not fall, because it had its foundation on the rock. But everyone who hears these words of mine and does not put them into practice is like a foolish man who built his house on sand. The rain came down, the streams rose, and the winds blew and beat against that house, and it fell with a great crash.*
> — Matthew 7:24-27

God wants us to build our lives on a firm foundation. That's why he speaks of putting these words into action, not just repeating them. That's why he speaks of putting these words in our hearts, not just on our lips. That's why he speaks of impressing his Law upon children, and talking about them in the home. That's why he speaks of taking these words along on our journey through life ("when you walk along the road") and to bed with us at night ("when you lie down"). That's why he speaks of repeating them early in the morning ("when you get up"), tying them to our wrists, wearing them on our foreheads, and writing them on the doorframes of our houses. Keeping these words about God being one and loving him with all of our hearts, souls, and strength gives us a foundation for the abundant life.

Does this sound like God wants us to follow his Law because he loves us? Of course it does. Let me put it another way. It is only possible for us to believe in the one and only God and love him because he first loved us. The command to love the Lord God is an invitation to love him back. God loves us. More importantly, God is love.

1 John 4:7-10 puts it this way:

> *Dear friends, let us love one another, for love comes from God. Everyone who loves has been born of God and knows God, because God is love. This is how God showed his love among us: He sent his one and only Son into the world that we might live through him. This is love: not that we loved God, but that he loved us and sent his Son as an atoning sacrifice for our sins. Dear friends, since God so loved us, we also ought to love one another. No one has ever seen God; but if we love one another, God lives in us and his love is made complete in us.*

The love of God for us precedes the Law of God. God gives us the Ten Commandments as an expression of his love for us. What is the motivation of a mother who tells her child not to put his hand into the fire on the stove because he will get burned? Isn't it love? What is the motivation of a father who tells his young daughter not to run out onto a busy highway? Isn't it love? In like manner, God tells us not to break his laws because if we do, we will get hurt or even killed. Like the parent of a young child, God knows what is best for us. Often we do not know. We think that we can play with fire or dodge cars on a busy highway, but we are wrong. When we realize that God forbids certain things because he loves us, we can embrace his commands.

The reason we are called to love God and his commands is that God loves us and wants only the best for us. We are blessed (happy) when we come to this realization. Psalm 112:1 puts it this way: "Praise the LORD! Happy are those who fear the LORD, who greatly delight in his commandments."

To fear the Lord does not mean being afraid of him, but having awe before him. Think of yourself standing at the bottom of the Grand Canyon. Now look up. What you feel is awe. What is around you is great and majestic. That is what the Bible means by fear. In the Bible, the fear of God doesn't mean being afraid of God. It means utter reverence and awe. Those who have this reverence delight in God's commands. That is why the Bible says that "the fear of the LORD is the beginning of wisdom" (Psalm 111:10).

Psalm 119:97 says, "Oh, how I love your law! It is my meditation all day long." Why do so many people resist God's laws today in contrast to the psalmist who loved God's ways? The answer lies in the lack of understanding of reverence for the Lord. You can only love the ways of God if you love the Lord God first.

Psalm 119:118 teaches that the Law of God is light for the dark paths ahead of us in life. "Your word is a lamp to my feet and a light to my path." Why do so many people resist God's word? Many are afraid that embracing the word of God means that their lives will be limited and circumscribed instead of free. The exact opposite is the case. Only as we love the Lord and his ways can we have a sure future and be the free children of God we were intended to be.

Psalm 119:152 shows us that to break the Law of God means being broken by that Law. "Long ago I learned from your decrees that you have established them forever," the wise psalmist wrote. The Ten Commandments are eternal. They will last until the end of time.

Contrary to modern belief, the Ten Commandments are not principles that were appropriate only for people long ago and far away. Contrary to the popular philosophy of ethical relativism, the Ten Commandments are established forever. Contrary to Joe Fletcher and his book *Situational Ethics*, the summary of the Ten Commandments to love the Lord and neighbor does not place the Ten Commandments on the shelf. Remember that Jesus himself said that he did not come to abolish the Law and the Prophets, but to fulfill them (Matthew 5:17).

We need both the Law and the gospel of love. The main purpose of the Law is to show us how we have sinned, leading to repentance. The clear purpose of the gospel of Jesus Christ is tell us that God hates our sins, but continues to love the sinner. The gospel does not replace the Law, but provides a way to overcome the guilt that comes when we realize that the Law condemns us.

Contrary to what most people seem to believe today, real guilt is good, not bad. Actually, there are two kinds of guilt. False guilt is not good. False guilt means feeling guilty when you have *not* done something wrong. False guilt feels like real guilt, but it comes from inferiority feelings, not sin. We all have some false guilt; some people are seriously inhibited by it. The resolution for false guilt is not repentance, but acceptance from God and people.

On the other hand, real guilt comes because we have hurt God by breaking his Law. Karl Menninger, the founder of the famous Menninger Institute, wrote *Whatever Became Of Sin?* This book raises the important question about the tendency in America to marginalize or eliminate sin from our vocabulary and our life by removing the category of sin altogether.

Both those who feel inferior and those who do not have an inferiority complex are guilty of sin. Sin is self-centeredness. "All have sinned and fallen short of the glory of God," the Bible teaches. Both those who feel inferior and those who do not feel inferior are sinners. Sins come from that basic human tendency of making ourselves the center of life. The Ten Commandments describe specific ways we offend God by our sins. Real guilt is only resolved by repentance by the sinner and forgiveness by God and people we have hurt.

Our generation seeks freedom from despotic domination. That is only as it should be, but in the process of trying to get away from human despots, we too easily forget the authority of God over us. The word "authority" comes from the word "author." An author has rights of ownership over what he or she has created. I have written twenty books. As an author of these books, I can submit them to a publisher or throw them into the trash. That is my right. God is the author of the universe and all the people on the earth. By definition, he has the right of authorship over us.

The basic creed of Christianity is "Jesus is Lord."[1] Jesus is no despot. He is a loving Lord. He rules over us for our own good, not because he has some twisted need to be adored. The basic call of Christianity is for people to see that they cannot save themselves and therefore submit their lives to the lordship of Christ. "It is God's nature to make something out of nothing," Martin Luther observed. "If you are not yet nothing, he can't make anything out of you." A recognition that we cannot get ourselves out of our own hands is the first step toward wholeness. The Ten Commandments, properly understood, help us to see our need for a Savior.

No act of the self can lift the self out of the self by the self because the self is the biggest problem we have. Our generation is caught in the extremes of self-determination, self-expression, and self-fulfillment. We need a Savior. We have a Savior in Jesus Christ. The Ten Commandments are invitations to discover our false image of the world and ourselves. Freed from illusions, we can turn to God's answer in his Son.

All people everywhere suffer from the dilemma of trying to save themselves. All fail because we can't save ourselves. All people everywhere are called to obedience to God and his commands. We all fall short because of our sinful nature. All people need Jesus Christ as Savior and Lord.

The Ten Commandments are found in the Bible. The Ten Commandments are also written in the hearts of all people. "The requirements of the law are written on their hearts" (Romans 2:15). All people everywhere need the Savior, God's own Son, Jesus Christ.

Jesus said, "Everyone who hears these words of mine (including my words about the Law and the Prophets) and puts them into practice will be like a wise man who built his house on the rock" (Matthew 7:24).

Before you can build a house from the ground up, you must build a foundation that gives stability to what goes above it. God has provided that stable foundation in the Law and the gospel. We neglect this foundation to our peril. If we pay attention to this foundation, try to follow God's Word, and repent when we fail, we will find that God delights in us. Deuteronomy 30:9b-14 puts it this way:

> *The Lord will again delight in you and make you prosperous, just as he delighted in your fathers, if you obey the Lord your God and keep his commands and decrees that are written in this Book of the Law and turn to the Lord your God with all your heart and with all your soul.*

Now what I am commanding you today is not too difficult for you or beyond your reach. It is not up in heaven, so that you have to ask, "Who will ascend into heaven to get it and proclaim it to us so we may obey it?" Nor is it beyond the sea, so that you have to ask, "Who will cross the sea to get it and proclaim it to us so we may obey it?" No, the word is very near you; it is in your mouth and in your heart so you may obey it.

* * *

Note

If you are studying this book in a group, discuss the meaning of these biblical foundations today. Also discuss the quote below.

More people act themselves
into right ways
of thinking
than think
themselves
into right ways of acting.
Therefore the question is not, "How much do you believe?" but "What are you willing to do about what you believe?"
— Ron Lavin

The Ten Commandments

The First Table
Of The Law

Chapter One

Prohibitions And Invitations In The First Commandment

And God spoke all these words:
I am the LORD your God, who brought you out of Egypt, out of the land of slavery. You shall have no other gods before me. — Exodus 20:1-2

The oldest problem in the world is idolatry. Idolatry is older than adultery. It is older than murder, stealing, and lying. Adam and Eve were caught in the web of idolatry when they disobeyed the clear order of God not to eat of the tree of knowledge of good and evil. They valued their own desires and thoughts higher than the command of God. To value something higher than God is the very nature of idolatry.

The sin of valuing something higher than God is the sin behind all other sins. Whatever is valued higher than God is a false god. The false god of Adam and Eve was their desire for what was forbidden. Sound familiar? They were sure that they knew better than God what was best for them. They believed in God. Their problem was that they wanted God to take a backseat to something they valued higher than God. Whenever we ask God to take a backseat, we break the First Commandment.

The Bible offers a diagnosis of the problem that leads to sickness and bondage. The Bible also offers a prescription for restoration of health and freedom.

Prohibitions Against Idolatry

"I don't believe in God," a man once said to a pastor.

The pastor thought for a moment and then replied, "Tell me about the god you don't believe in. Chances are, I don't believe in that god either." The god people don't believe in is a god who causes suffering and pain. Christians don't believe in that god, either. The god people renounce is the god who causes wars between nations and relatives. That god is not God. When people say, "I don't believe in God," they often mean they don't believe in a policeman-like god who delights in trying to catch them in their mistakes or a judge-like god who is ruthlessly trying to punish them. The god people say they don't believe in is usually not the God and Father of our Lord Jesus Christ. The god people renounce is generally not the one true God.

It is important to know what people are renouncing. Christians renounce all human illusions about God. Illusions are false ideas. We need to be freed from our false ideas about God. Jesus came to earth to give us the true picture of what the one, true God is like.

Since the biblical teaching is that there is only one true God, the real question is not, "Do you believe in God?" but "In which God do you believe — the one true God or a god you make up which is not God?" God made us so that we would worship him as the highest good in our lives. If we don't put God in first place, we will put something else there. Whatever else we place in first place in our lives — that something or someone is an idol.

Idolatry is worshiping false gods. A false god is any thing or any person that is at the center of my life. We have no trouble condemning the worship of the man-made gods of ancient times. The golden calf made by the ancient Hebrews is easy to renounce. We have much more trouble seeing the false gods of our times. Anything, good or evil, which comes to occupy the center of my life, other than the one true God, is an idol which must be renounced.

What are some of the idols of our time? How about
- success?
- status?
- celebrities?

- money?
- vehicles?
- science?
- knowledge?

Many of these things are good. They just are not intended to be the center of my life. Below God, some of these things can be meaningful and helpful. As a center of life, modern idols don't work.

How about
- the pursuit of happiness?
- the pursuit of a healthy body?
- a job?
- a spouse?
- children?

These things are good when they are placed below God, but do not work as the number one thing in our lives. Only God is God. Everything else we put in first place leads to disaster, even if that thing is a spouse or a child. A spouse gets sick and dies. A child leaves home. Only God remains forever.

God made us so that we will not work right unless he is right in the center of our lives. "I am the LORD your God. You shall have no other gods before me." False gods will not do. Generation after generation rises and falls making the same mistake of trying to put something ahead of God. Year after year the repeated problem of idolatry causes troubles on troubles.

The prophets repeatedly faced this problem. Moses, Elijah, Jeremiah, Isaiah, Exekiel, Amos, Hosea, and Micah all stormed against the idolatry of their day, but the worship of false gods raised it's ugly head time and again. Let's look at three of these prophets in the Old Testament and a story in the New Testament. These stories demonstrate the evils of idolatry.

When Moses came down from Mount Sinai where he had received the Ten Commandments, he found the Hebrews gathered around the golden calf they had erected while Moses was away. Moses crashed to the ground the stones on which the Commandments were written. The people were severely punished for making the image of a false god. We make false gods because the one true God doesn't do what we want him to do or he doesn't act on our timetable. We easily fall into the trap of thinking that the one true God is not available when we need him. When we trust someone or something other than the one true God as the center of our lives, troubles compound.

Elijah railed against the false Baal god and the idolaters of his day. Do you remember the challenge he offered at the time of a drought? At Mount Carmel the prophet of Yahweh, the one true God, challenged the prophets of false gods by asking them to call down fire from the heavens. When their attempt to call down fire failed, Elijah asked, "Are your gods asleep?" Then Elijah prayed to Yahweh. Fire came and soon the long sought rain came as well. False gods are always asleep. False gods can never help us. False gods are not God.

Ezekiel received the word of God and was told to swallow the scroll on which God's word was written. The food he needed to sustain him when he faced the idolatry of his day was God's word. He was told, "Go to your countrymen in exile and speak to them. Say to them, 'This is what the Sovereign LORD says,' whether they listen or fail to listen" (Ezekiel 3:11). The truth of God will stand no matter how many people refuse to believe it. The Lord alone is sovereign.

In the New Testament we learn of the idolatry of Matthew the tax collector. Matthew had betrayed his fellow Jews by becoming a tax collector for Rome. He had to collect a certain amount of money for Rome. Anything over that amount he could keep as his salary. He lined his pockets with unrighteous mammon at the expense of his fellow countrymen because he made money his god. When Jesus came his way and called out, "Follow me," Matthew left his tax booth and followed him. When Jesus was criticized for associating with Matthew and other tax collectors, he said, "It is not the healthy that need a doctor, but sinners. I did not come to invite the virtuous people, but sinners." Like Matthew, God calls us away from false loyalties that make us sick. He calls us to follow him.

Invitations To Health And Freedom

Let's look at Matthew and Isaiah as they experienced repentance and returned to God who brings health and freedom. Idolatrous Matthew became Saint Matthew, the apostle. He took the prescription that Jesus, the divine physician, offered. Matthew reordered his life and became a new man. Reordering your life under God is what Martin Luther means when he says in *The Small Catechism* that we should fear, love, and trust God above all things.[2] That's God's prescription for health and freedom.

Proverbs 1:7 says, "The fear of God is the beginning of knowledge." The fear of God is different than being afraid of God. Fear of God means awe or utter respect for God. Fear of God means reverence for God. In your imagination, go to the bottom of the Sears Tower. Now, look up. What you see is so much bigger than you are that awe fills your being. The fear of God is like that. The fear of God is humility before the almighty.

Humility doesn't mean crunching down and pretending to be less than you are. True humility means standing at your full stature before something so much greater than you that you feel overwhelmed by the experience. The fear of God is about *true humility.*

The fear of God means that we are overwhelmed by the lordship of God. God can do what he sees fit, yet he chooses to love us. God has absolute freedom, yet in that freedom he chooses to enter human flesh in the person of Jesus to save us. God is the initiator; we just react to him. He initiates the relationship with us by loving us when we are not worthy. His love is overwhelming. We are called to respond by loving him back.

Matthew, the tax collector, was overwhelmed by Jesus. He sensed the power and authority of Jesus. When Jesus said, "Follow me," Matthew followed. The fear of God came into his heart. The love of God flooded his heart. He reordered his life by putting God in first place.

Isaiah, the prophet, also experienced the fear and love of God.

> *In the year that King Uzziah died, I saw the Lord seated on a throne, high and exalted and the train of his robe filled the temple. Above him were seraphs, each with*

> six wings: With two wings they covered their faces, with two they covered their feet, and with two they were flying. And they were calling to one another: "Holy, holy, holy is the LORD Almighty; the whole earth is full of his glory."
> At the sound of their voices the doorposts and thresholds shook and the temple was filled with smoke.
> "Woe is me!" I cried. "I am ruined. For I am a man of unclean lips, and I live among a people of unclean lips and my eyes have seen the King, the LORD Almighty."
> — Isaiah 6:1-5

That's what the fear of God is like. Initially it is a feeling of being found out, ruined or undone. Then comes forgiveness and affirmation of value. Both Matthew and Isaiah experienced awe before God. Then they were sent on a mission for God. "Follow me," Jesus said to Matthew. "Whom shall I send? Who will go for us?" God asked Isaiah. "Here I am. Send me!" Isaiah responded.

The fear of God means a radical *relocation* of authority. Our problem today might be called the radical *dislocation* of authority. In making ourselves, instead of God, the measure of all things, we suffer the consequences of a breakdown of educational systems, institutions, and the family. The prescription for our society as well as for individuals is the *relocation* of authority in the one true God. The restoration of the fear of God results in love for God. This is the only solution to idolatry, the oldest problem in the world.

Don't believe the common assumption that coming under God's authority inhibits us. Actually it frees us. Freedom from God is bondage. Bondage to God is freedom. We were created to know the health, wholeness, and unlimited love of God as king and to respond by loving God in return with our hearts, minds, souls, and strength. When that happens, we are free from bondage. The First Commandment says,

> I am the LORD your God, who brought you out of Egypt, out of the land of slavery. You shall have no other gods before me.
> — Exodus 20:2

Questions For Your Personal And/Or Group Consideration

1. How would you answer someone who says, "I don't believe in God"? Consider the positive aspects of replying, "Tell me about the god you don't believe in. Chances are I don't believe in that god either."

2. An idol is _____.

3. In the light of the biblical concept of the fear of God, consider the statement, "What looks like freedom is bondage and what looks like bondage is freedom."

4. When people come up with rules for us, it is fitting to ask, "What's in it for them?" When God gives us his Commandments, what's in it for him? Check off the answers below that you consider correct.
   ____ Ruling over us so that he will feel omnipotent
   ____ Our wholeness
   ____ Our peace
   ____ Our freedom to use our gifts for God.

5. A child once said, "The First Commandment was when Eve told Adam to eat the apple." Any comments?

6. A kite once said to a bird, "I'm bound by this string. Help me." When the bird chewed the string and freed the kite, that freedom led to the destruction of the kite. Any comments?

Digging Deeper

1. Consider John 14:6 which answers the question, "Won't any old god do?"

2. Read Acts 4:12 which answers the question, "By what power or by what name did you do this (healing)?"

3. Read Acts 16:16-31 about Paul and Silas.
   What was their command to the unclean spirit? _____

   What did they say in answer to the question, "Sirs, what must I do to be saved?" _____
   _____

4. One of the forms of idolatry in our day is astrology; horoscopes and signs. A new convert was asked this question at a party: "What is your sign?" How would you answer this question?

   The new convert answered this way: "My sign is the sign of the cross."

5. If you are in a group, discuss Luther's explanation of the First Commandment: "We are to fear, love, and trust God above everything else."

6. Robert Tuttle has described the Commandments as a narrow runway at an airport.[3] "Land here and you will be safe. Try to land in front of this runway, or behind it, or on the side of it and you will crash." If you are in a group, discuss this idea.

Chapter Two

Prohibitions And Invitations In The Second Commandment

You shall not misuse the name of the LORD your God, for the LORD will not hold him guiltless who misuses his name. — Exodus 20:7

If you are a Christian, you were baptized "In the name of the Father, the Son, and the Holy Spirit." These words mean that you have been set aside as one of God's children. To be baptized also means that you are God's ambassador. God has a name. The way you use that name and represent that name indicates what you think of God.

As Christians, our home is not on this earth, but *in* heaven. We live in this world, but we are not *of* this world. This world is a foreign country. We are God's ambassadors in a foreign land. We represent God and his name.

A general and his wife were walking down the street of a foreign country one day when they saw a private who was drunk lying in the gutter. His shirt was unbuttoned. His uniform was dirty. The general excused himself, walked over to the soldier and said, "How dare you! You represent the United States of America! Now get back to the barracks and clean yourself up."

In like manner, we represent the kingdom of God. We are called to represent God in this foreign land called the world. We represent him by our words and deeds.

Prohibitions Against Using God's Name In Vain

The Second Commandment does not condemn the use of crude words like "hell" or "damn" in our speech. I am not urging the use of these crude words, I am just trying to point out that when it comes to the way we speak, the second Commandment condemns the misuse of God's name. Let me put it a different way. Any time the name "God," "Lord," "Jesus," "Christ," or any derivative thereof, comes out of my mouth without having gone with reverence through my heart as an act of worship, praying, teaching, or preaching, I have broken the Second Commandment and deserve to be severely punished. God's name is important. God said so. We can trust his word that those who misuse his name are guilty of a grave sin.

Before Moses received the Second Commandment from God on Mount Sinai, he encountered God in a burning bush. God told him to return to Egypt from which he had fled. God told him to lead his people out of bondage. After much protest about his inability to speak and lead, Moses finally agreed to go back to Egypt for God, but first, he said, he needed to know God's proper name because the people would ask him for it.

The answer God gave Moses cannot be translated into English. If we transliterate the Hebrew letters into English, the name God gave Moses comes out JHWH. The Hebrews were so respectful of God's proper name that they never used it in speech. The name was written down and passed on from generation to generation, but for many years the Hebrew language had no vowels. Therefore, after some time passed, no one knew how to pronounce the name God gave to Moses. Later, when scholars added vowels to the Hebrew language, they had to guess what vowels to add and where to add them. For a time people thought that the name of God was pronounced Jehovah. Today most scholars say that this is not the correct pronunciation of the name God gave Moses on Mount Sinai. Today scholars think that the proper pronunciation is "Yahweh." Actually, we don't know the proper pronunciation of God's proper name as given to Moses.

The point of all this is that for fear of offending God by misusing his name, the early Hebrews didn't speak it at all. Compare

that with today. God's holy name is dragged through the muck and the mire every day at:
- school,
- factories,
- offices,
- locker rooms,
- barbershops and hairdresser shops,
- and the homes of our land.

Count the number of times you hear the name of God taken in vain this next week. I have challenged confirmation students to do just that. The number they counted often reached well beyond a hundred in just one week and these students come from Christian homes. Compare modern misuse of God's name to the psalmist who said, "O LORD, our Lord, how majestic is your name in all the earth" (Psalm 8:1).

A Christian friend who works in the construction industry stated: "Contrary to popular belief, God's last name is not 'Damn.'" Another friend said that before she was converted to Christ, the only way she heard God's name was in swearing and cursing.

How we use God's name indicates what we think of God. If we use God's name in worship and prayer, that means that we respect God. If we use God's name in private and public worship, preaching the gospel and teaching Christianity to others, that means we honor God. On the other hand, if we drag God's name in the mud by damning someone with it or use it loosely in everyday speech with no intention of respect or honor, that means that we do not recognize God's holiness in our speech.

Disrespect for God's name means disrespect for God. We are not just abusing God's name in our society; we are showing utter disrespect for God himself. The name and the person go together. If I used your name in vain, wouldn't you be offended? Of course you would. You wouldn't say, "He's just talking about my name, not me." When we are thoughtless and insensitive about God's name, we are thoughtless and insensitive about God.

The excuse that "I don't mean anything by it; it's just a bad habit" won't wash. Using God's name in vain may be a bad habit, but it is not *just* a bad habit. It is an insult. That's why God says that this sin will not go unpunished.

An Army chaplain was listening to two soldiers talk outside his tent. First one, then the other, told filthy stories and used God's name in vain time and again. Finally the chaplain could take it no more. He went to the door of his tent and said, "Stop your filthy speech. You are talking about someone I love."

Sometimes the Second Commandment is broken because someone is trying to show off and appear to be a bigger man or woman than he/she is. When I was thirteen years old, five years before I was a Christian, I went through a period when I used God's name in vain frequently. I heard adults do it. I thought that it made me sound like a big man. At age eighteen, when I became a Christian, I looked back with a heavy heart on this sin as well as others. Trying to show off, I was hurting the Lord by my words and deeds. Showing off is childish.

Saint Paul said, "When I became a man, I put away childish things." As a new Christian that verse hit me right between the eyes. I said in prayer, "I'm really sorry, Father. I deserve your punishment for breaking the Second Commandment. I thank you for Jesus Christ and that he died on the cross for my sins, and I promise you that I will make every effort to clean up my speech."

Even saying "I'm sorry" to God can be a way of breaking the Second Commandment, if the one who says it is insincere, or just trying to avoid punishment. If saying "I'm sorry," is not based on genuine remorse, we trivialize God. To trivialize God in prayer is to take his name in vain. If we have no intention of straightening up our act, and thoughtlessly repeat sinful actions, we are further estranged from God.

What if I blame God for my troubles? That, too, can be a way of breaking the Second Commandment. You have heard the big question that comes up when things go wrong. You've probably said it. "Why did God do this to me?" That question means that we are trying to hold God responsible for the evil and frustrating things that happen in our lives.

A "prim and proper" Christian often prayed something like this: "Deareth Godeth, I'eth loveth youeth. I willeth followeth youeth no matter what lifeth bringeth."

Then his world caved in. He could not handle what happened to him. He was filled with anger and frustration and he prayed quite differently than before.

He prayed: "God, why did you do this to me?"

God answered, "Not meeth. Youeth."

Gert Behanna, a spoiled rich woman, went through alcoholism, drug addiction, three divorces, and a failed suicide attempt before she turned her life over to Christ. She also turned her sins, including those against the Second Commandment, over to Christ. In hindsight, she said, "I can damn God, but God is not damned. I can belittle his house, but his house is not belittled."

Damning God does not make God less holy; it makes us less holy. Damning another person using God's name, does not damn that person; it places us on the slippery slope that leads to darkness where demonic forces rule.

Ungodly speech based on thoughtlessness, showing off, blaming God for our troubles, or damning God or people in God's name indicates a lack of respect for God's holiness. On the other hand, we must remember that it is always God's intention to restore us to a proper relationship with him. The purpose of illustrating the many ways we break the Second Commandment in speech is not to leave us in our sin. On the contrary, the fact that we are convicted before this and all the Commandments means that we are shown the way of release from our sins through repentance and faith in Christ.

Martin Luther explained the meaning of the second Commandment like this:

> *We should so fear and love God that we do not curse, swear, conjure, lie, or deceive by his name, but call upon him in every time of need, and worship him with prayer, praise, and thanksgiving.*[4]

We are not perfect; but are we capable of seeing what we have done wrong and starting again with God. This Commandment shows us our imperfections in speech. It also shows us our imperfections in deeds.

Prohibitions Against Certain Deeds

Remember, baptism makes us God's children and God's ambassadors on earth. If we don't act like God's children, our deeds are a bad reflection on our Father. If by our deeds we are bad ambassadors for God, people will not know what God is really like. To respect and honor God means to display through our lives our words of belief. To respect and honor God means that we try to give glory to God by the way we talk and the way we walk our talk.

Actions speak so loudly that people can hardly hear what we are saying if those actions do not express our faith. Soren Kierkegaard once said that we have too many "parade-ground Christians" who wear the uniform, or appearance, of believing but never do battle on behalf of the faith. Jeremiah, the prophet, puts it like this:

> *Behold, you trust in deceptive words to no avail. Will you steal, murder, commit adultery, swear falsely, burn incense to Baal, and go after other gods that you have not known, and then come and stand before me in this house, which is called by my name, and say, "We are delivered' — only to go on doing all these abominations? Has this house, which is called by my name, become a den of robbers in your eyes? Behold, I myself have seen it," says the Lord.*
> — Jeremiah 7:9-11 (RSV)

Gross inconsistencies between what we say on Sunday mornings and what we do the rest of the week are seen by God. It is one thing to become a Christian. It is another to live as a Christian. Of course, no matter how hard we try to live the Christian life, we will fail time and again. No matter how sincere we are in our repentance, we will continue to be sinners. But shouldn't we be trying to live like Christ and sincerely repent when we fall short? Isn't there something true to the charge of outsiders that there are hypocrites in the church today, just as surely as there were hypocrites in Jesus' day?

Sins of the flesh like adultery, fornication, and lust are bad enough, but how about the more subtle sins like a judgmental spirit, envy, pride, and jealousy? If you think that you are free from sins, consider the words of Gert Behanna, who was mentioned earlier in this chapter: "I've just discovered a new sin. I look down on people who look down on people."

Our sins of commission are great. How about our sins of omission? There are many things we should be doing that we overlook. Let me illustrate that point personally. I am an intense person. When I set my mind to doing something, I really focus on it. Having a strong focus isn't all bad, but neither is it all good. There is a negative side to having an intense focus. I often miss people by the side of the road. That is the problem of the priest and the Levite in the story of the good Samaritan. Too often, I am guilty of missing people with needs. I often just don't see them until someone points them out.

I'm working on my problem of being too intense. I hope that at least I'm not as bad as I was when my wife and I first got married. I was a senior at Carthage College at the time. When I was studying, I needed quiet in the house. I requested that no television or radio be on, even in another room. One night when I was studying for a Greek exam, I heard a lot of noise coming from the front room. I rushed out and asked, "What's all that noise?" To my embarrassment, my wife Joyce replied, "Noise? I'm just knitting a sweater."

On another occasion, I was leading a retreat for teenagers. In the middle of the night, the fire went out. It was dark and cold. We were all sleeping on the floor in sleeping bags. I struggled with whether or not to stay in my warm sleeping bag or get up and put some more logs on the fire. "Do the Christian thing," a voice in my head said. I got up and steadfastly headed for the fireplace, trying to do the right thing. On the way, I stepped on the head of one of the boys. Sometimes, even when we try to do a good deed, we hurt other people. That's why we need a Savior.

Invitations To A New Life

Christians are not perfect. If the truth be known, much of the time we are not even good. We are sinners and saints. Through Christ we are restored to the state of being "a little lower than angels." This Commandment and the Bible deal with more than our need for a Savior. Among other things, this Commandment means we are called to be God's representatives on earth.

Baptism has made us ambassadors for the Lord Jesus Christ. By baptism and grace, the Holy Spirit is at work in us fashioning us after the likeness of Christ, making us better messengers for the kingdom.

My friend Gert Behanna, a recovering alcoholic, became a great ambassador for God. She spoke to thousands of people all over the world, using the title "God Isn't Dead." She told her story of conversion and inspired many to turn their selfish lives over to God.

Gert always ended her talk by using this prayer: "O God, we aren't what we ought to be. And God, we aren't what we're going to be. But thanks God, because we aren't what we used to be."

Because of God's grace and the faith he creates in our hearts, we aren't what we used to be. We are ambassadors for Christ living in a foreign land, the world. We are invited to represent God to others with a new way to think, talk, and act.

Questions For Your Personal Consideration And/Or Group Discussion

1. Is the concept of Christians as ambassadors in a foreign land helpful? Explain.

2. Why do people use God's name in vain?

3. Why don't we know the pronunciation of YHWH, the name God gave to Moses?

4. Count the number of times you hear the name of God taken in vain this next week and report the total to your group or class members when you next meet.

5. Do you agree or disagree with the statement, "The excuse that people don't mean anything by using God's name in vain and that it is just a bad habit is unacceptable to Christians." Explain.

6. How can saying, "I'm sorry" to God be breaking the Second Commandment?

7. What does Gert Behanna's prayer at the end of this chapter mean?

Digging Deeper

1. "Name" is often used in Hebrew in the sense of revealed character and essence. God swears by his great name to carry out his purpose (Jeremiah 44:26), that is, he swears by his attested power to accomplish his word. The name of God which is excellent in all the earth (Psalm 8:1) is that expression of his being which is exhibited in creation and redemption.[5]

2. The English word "God" is derived from a root meaning "to call," and indicates simply the object of worship, one whom men call upon or invoke. The Greek word which it translates in the pages of the New Testament, however, describes this object of worship as Spirit; and the Old Testament Hebrew word, which this word in turn represents, conveys, as its primary meaning, the idea of power. On Christian lips, therefore, the word God designates the almighty Spirit who is worshiped.[6]

3. The nature of God has been made known to men in three planes of revelation: first as the infinite spirit or the God of nature; then as the redeemer of sinners, or the God of grace; and lastly as the Father, Son, and Holy Ghost (Spirit), or Triune God.[7]

4. YHWH is generally translated "I AM" or "I AM WHO AM."

5. Gert Behanna is mentioned several times in this chapter. Her story is told in her book *The Late Liz*, and in a motion picture by the same title starring Ann Bancroft.

6. Read 2 Corinthians 5:20 where Saint Paul speaks of himself and his fellow workers as Christ's ambassadors.

Chapter Three

Prohibitions And Invitations In The Third Commandment

Remember the Sabbath day by keeping it holy.
— Exodus 20:8

Remember that you were slaves in Egypt and that the LORD your God brought you out of there with a mighty hand and an outstretched arm. Therefore the LORD your God has commanded you to observe the Sabbath day. — Deuteronomy 5:15

"What's so special about your Sabbath day?" a young man asked his girlfriend. He was an unbeliever; she a faithful Christian. He did not go to church. She attended each Sunday. "Why do you go to church?" he asked.

She paused for a moment. Then she replied, "God commanded it; therefore I try to do it. Worship meets a deep need in my heart." At the time, he did not accept her answer. Later, when he became a Christian, he understood what she had meant. As a Christian, he described his pre-Christian days like this: "There was a hole in my soul that only God could fill, but before I became a Christian I didn't know that only God could fill that hole." Worship means filling the hole in our souls.

Saint Augustine said, "Restless is my soul until it find rest in thee." Worship is a way we find rest for our restless souls.

Worship is also a way to come before the Lord with awe and love. Martin Luther puts it this way: "We are to fear and love God so that we do not neglect his Word and the preaching of it, but regard it as holy and gladly hear and learn it."[8] The fear of God does not mean that we are afraid of God, but that we have awe for God. In the preaching and the teaching of God's Word and receiving God's sacraments we have an opportunity to be humbled (filled with awe) before God and express our love for him.

In the Exodus and Deuteronomy passages cited at the beginning of this chapter, we hear that we are to remember the one who first loved us. In the Exodus passage, we are urged to remember our loving Creator; in the Deuteronomy passage that we are to remember our loving Redeemer. What is so special about the Sabbath day? It is a day of remembrance and redemption.

Remembrance

In his book *The Living Reminder*, Henri Nouwen, a Roman Catholic writer about spirituality, says, "To remember is not simply to look back at past events; more importantly, it is to bring these events into the present and celebrate them here and now. For Israel, remembrance means participation."[9] He goes on to explain that in the Bible remembrance means to actualize events and persons of the past. Concretely, to remember the Sabbath day means to actualize God's creative work at the beginning of time. It also means to actualize God's creation of each of us.

Let's look at seven ways that remembering God in worship actualizes God for us. First, we worship on the Sabbath day so that we remember that God is God and that we are his created children. Sometimes we forget who God is and act like we are in control of our own lives. In other words, God commanded us to worship him that we might remember who created us and that we belong to him. We are called to behave like the children of our loving Father.

Second, we are called to worship God because God knows that if we do not worship him, we will put something, or someone else, in his place. We do not have a choice of whether or not we will worship; only who will be the object of our worship. In other words, if we don't worship the one true God, we will put someone else or something else in first place in our lives. Nothing but God works as the highest value in our lives. Everything but God disappoints as the ultimate ruler. Without God in first place, we will discover that life is just "sound and fury, signifying nothing," as Shakespeare wrote.

Third, God commanded us to worship him because worship is the way of knowing who we are by discovering whose we are. We are lost children, wandering in the wilderness of life, seeking for meaning and direction. Worshiping God, our Creator, is a way of discovering and rediscovering our created purpose which is to glorify God and enjoy him throughout our lives.

Fourth, we are called to remember and celebrate the Sabbath day so we remember that we had a beginning and that we will have an ending. Whether we live to be 25 or 95, we are limited creatures. Those who do not worship God regularly forget that they have only a short span of life on earth and that eternity is forever. Worship reminds us that this life is a preparation for eternity.

Fifth, God commanded us to remember the Sabbath day so that we can get in touch with the reverence he placed in our hearts at our creation. Oliver Wendell Holmes, the famous jurist, put it this way, "There is a little plant called 'reverence' within me, and it needs to be watered regularly, about one day in seven."

Sixth, to remember God through Sabbath worship is to afford ourselves an opportunity for re-creation. We work in the world that teaches justification by works. If we produce, we are rewarded. We need to be reminded that the opposite is true with God. With God we are justified by what he has done. With God we are not achievers, but receivers. We are called to produce good works for God, not to justify ourselves, but because God has done so much for us. To remember our Creator through worship is to be re-created to face the world and work with a higher perspective on the meaning of life.

Seventh, God gave us the Sabbath day for worship in order that we might see things the way they really are instead of as they seem to be. In Psalm 73 we read about a devout man who was confused by the fact that unrighteous and self-centered people seemed to be prospering and those who loved God seemed to be fools and failures. Then the psalmist went to the sanctuary and got the higher perspective on how things really are.[10]

> *But as for me, my feet had almost stumbled, my steps had well nigh slipped. For I was envious of the arrogant, when I saw the prosperity of the wicked ... Behold, these are the wicked; always as ease, they increase in riches. All in vain have I kept my heart clean and washed my hands in innocence ... When I thought how to understand this, it seemed to me a wearisome task, until I went into the sanctuary of God, and perceived their end.* — Psalm 73:2-17 (RSV)

It was only in the sanctuary of God that the psalmist got the higher perspective that the unrighteous die and will have to face judgment before God. He also learned that in life we sometimes have to say, "Nevertheless." In spite of things that happen, we are called to continue with faith in God.

> *When my soul was embittered, when I was pricked in heart, I was stupid and ignorant, I was like a beast toward thee. Nevertheless I am continually with thee; thou dost hold my right hand.* — Psalm 73:21-23 (RSV)

In worship, we can see the way things really are instead of how they seem to be. There we can learn to say, "Nevertheless, I am continually with thee."

Of course, every Sunday in church we do not experience these seven ways God can be actualized for us. Sometimes we hit dry seasons when we seem out of touch with God. Sometimes worship can seem dry or dead.

Two boys were standing in front of a plaque in church. "What is this?" the younger boy asked. "This is a plaque to remember the men who died in the service," said the older boy. The younger boy responded, "Which service — 8:00, 9:30, or 11:00?"

Sometimes worship may seem that it is a place for the dead instead of the living. Pastors and worship leaders must always seek to make worship services vital and related to the lives of the people who attend worship. Pastors and worship leaders must do all that they can to help worshipers remember the Father, Son, and Holy Spirit.

Redemption

The first giving of the Ten Commandments is recorded in Exodus. There we hear that the reason for keeping the Sabbath day holy is that God is our Creator. In Deuteronomy, when the Ten Commandments are repeated, a second reason to keep the Third Commandment is added. The second reason to worship is to remember that "you were slaves in Egypt and God brought you out of there....." In other words, we are called to celebrate Sabbath day worship because God is our Redeemer as well as our Creator.

God led the chosen people out of Egypt. "Remember that," Moses said from Mount Nebo, "and worship your Redeemer each Sabbath. Once you were slaves. Now you are free. God paid the price. He led you out of bondage."

The early Christians changed the day of worship from Saturday, the seventh day of the week, to Sunday, the first day of the week. The reason is that the resurrection of Jesus was the most important event in history. Easter happened on a Sunday. Easter was the day when Jesus conquered sin, death, and the devil. Therefore, for Christians, each Sunday is a day to remember our redemption. Each Sunday, God offers opportunities for us to leave slavery and enjoy the life of freedom God has prepared for us.

Let me say that again in a different way. The means of grace are available in church for our redemption. The means of grace are the preaching of the Word of God and the holy sacraments of Baptism and Holy Communion. These are channels from heaven to earth. These are God's ways of redemption. By these means of grace, God intends to give us new life by conquering sin (by offering us forgiveness), death (by promising eternal life to those who believe), and the devil (by giving us strength to resist the temptations of the evil one and to come back to him by repentance when we fail to resist). In other words, every Sunday is a little Easter.

We are called to actualize the Sabbath by remembering our Redeemer. Jesus died on the cross that we might have life and have it in abundance. He has provided the way we can meet him and receive his gifts through the word and sacraments. He promises to come to us through the means of grace.

Isn't it possible that we might meet Jesus at a lake while we are fishing on Sunday? Of course. Isn't it possible that we might meet him on the golf course? Yes. Couldn't we meet God in nature, by a stream, or on a mountaintop? Yes, but we are called to meet God where he has promised to be in his means of grace. God has promised that we will meet him in his word and his sacraments. Since he is going to be there, shouldn't we be there, too? It is when we are gathered together, as in church, that we have the assurance of the presence of the Redeemer. To neglect worshiping God in church is neglecting God's invitation to meet him where he promises to be.

Sunday is the first day of the week. Sunday worship can help us actualize the fact that God is first in our lives. Christians start each week with worship to show that God is their highest priority.

Some churches have made it possible for people to worship God on Saturday night. This is particularly helpful for those who have to work or who are traveling on Sunday. As long as the word and sacraments are available at Saturday night services, these services, like Sunday services, offer Sabbath worship for the people of God.

Our Roman Catholic brothers and sisters speak of Sunday as "a holy day of obligation." In a certain sense, that is true. After all, we are commanded to worship. On the other hand, it seems more helpful to speak of worship as an opportunity, not just a duty. The dictionary defines an opportunity as "a favorable conjunction of events and circumstances for doing something." The Sabbath opportunity is the favorable conjunction of your life with God's life. God takes the opportunity to be present with us in worship. We are invited to do the same. *Sunday is a holy day of opportunity.*

The prohibitions related to the Third Commandment are clear. We are told that Sunday is a holy day for worship. When we neglect regular worship, we break this Commandment. But the Third Commandment is also a clear invitation to keep God's Sabbath day holy by worshiping him. That's why I like the concept of *a holy day of opportunity.*

We began this chapter with the story of a young man and young woman. At the time of their initial conversation about worship he cynically asked, "What's so special about the Sabbath? Why do you worship?" She responded, "God commanded it and it meets a deep need in my heart." Later when he became a Christian, he could see that in his early life he had had a hole in his soul that only God could fill. Worship fills that hole.

I know. I am the former cynic who asked, "What's so special about the Sabbath?"

Questions For Your Personal Consideration And/Or Group Discussion

1. Saint Augustine said, "Restless is my soul until it find rest in thee." What does this mean?

2. Discuss this statement about worship:
    To worship is to quicken the conscience by the holiness of God;
    To feed the mind with the truth of God;
    To purge the imagination by the purity of God;
    To open the heart to the love of God;
    To devote the will to the purpose of God.

3. Discuss the meaning of remembrance as explained by Henri Nouwen in this chapter.

4. What does it mean to actualize God's creative and redemptive work?

5. What can be said to the person who claims to be too busy to go to church?

6. If you were planning a worship service, what would you want to be sure to include? What would you not include?

7. Some churches have dropped confession from their worship services. Do you agree or disagree with this practice? Why?

8. Read and consider John 9:13-41. This passage describes the Sabbath day controversy between Jesus and the spiritually blind Pharisees.

Digging Deeper

1. Consider the meaning of Acts 2:42-43, "They [the early Christians] devoted themselves to the apostles' teaching and to the fellowship, to the breaking of bread and to prayer. Everyone was filled with awe, and many wonders and miraculous signs were done by the apostles."

2. Read Psalm 73 and consider again the words of the psalmist, "Nevertheless, I am continually with thee."

3. Worship includes recognition, repentance, and redemption.
   Recognition means that we are aware of our condition as sinners. We can't lift ourselves out of ourselves by ourselves because we ourselves are the problem. Recognition means that we become aware of God as our only hope since we cannot achieve what needs to be done for our salvation. Recognition

means that we confess Jesus Christ as Lord of our lives and as our Savior.

Repentance means turning back to God. We are so easily led in the wrong directions. We know that we have hurt our Father by our thoughts and behavior. We want to return home to the Father.

Redemption means that Jesus' work on the cross has accomplished what needs to be done for us. Our role is to appropriate what has been accomplished. We appropriate what has been accomplished by faith in Christ.

The Ten Commandments

The Second Table
Of The Law

Chapter Four

Prohibitions And Invitations In The Fourth Commandment

Honor your father and your mother, so that you may live long in the land the LORD your God is giving you.
— Exodus 20:12

The first table of the Law (Commandments One through Three) deals with our relationship with God. God alone is God. He has a name. He has a day. Our devotion to him alone is the highest good. The way we use his name and the way we use his day indicate our relationship or lack of relationship with him.

The second table of the Law (Commandments Four through Ten) deals with human relationships. The very first Commandment in the second table is about the family. We learn how to relate, or how not to relate, to other people in our families. The watchwords for this Commandment about the family are honor and respect.

It may help to look at the Fourth Commandment about the family by using a square as a model. Consider the four sides of the family square shown on the next page.

```
                    (1) Honor parents
        ┌─────────────────────┐
        │                     │
(4) Holy home    FAMILY      (2) Honor all in
        │                     │    authority
        │                     │
        └─────────────────────┘
         (3) Honor and respect lead to
             quality and quantity of life
```

The first side of the family square is honor and respect for parents. This is the clear and fundamental meaning of the Fourth Commandment. Honor and respect don't mean absolute obedience. That is reserved for God alone. Parents, like children, are sinners. They make mistakes. For their own good, this Commandment calls upon children to look to their parents with reverence and when they are small, seek to follow what they are told. When the children are adults, this word from God calls upon them to treat parents with respect.

The Fourth Commandment calls parents to be honorable. Parents who lie or cheat or commit adultery easily forget that the children are watching. The holy home is built on parents who, while they are not perfect, seek to have integrity in their words and deeds.

The second side of the square is honoring all who are in authority. In *The Small Catechism*, Martin Luther points out that this Commandment calls us to respect, obey, love, and serve all those in authority over us. Of course, this obedience to those who are over us in the orders of society is not absolute obedience. Absolute obedience is reserved for God alone, but we are called to honor and respect all in authority in church, school, government, and other areas of our lives unless they violate our covenant with God as the highest authority. When those in positions of authority violate their trust, and try to order us to do the same, we are called to obey God rather than man (Acts 4:18-20).

Those in places of authority are called to show obedience to God and have integrity in behavior. This Commandment calls all who are in places of responsibility in the orders of society to be honorable. A father who lies, a pastor who is immoral, or a president who commits adultery, will have to answer to God for misleading those for whom they are responsible.

The third side of the family square is the promise of long life to those who honor and respect their elders. Does this promise really mean that those who follow this Command will live longer than those who do not? No, that clearly is not the case. Many disobedient people live long lives. Many who love God and his Commandments die early. One possibility is that this promise of long life means that if you show honor and respect in your family, you will live longer than you would if you neglect to show that honor and respect. Conflict in the family often gets internalized and causes sickness. Stress can hasten death, but is it just the quantity of days that increases when we heed this admonition? I don't think so. I think that obeying this Commandment includes quality as well as quantity of days. When there is a clear intention of showing honor and respect for those over us — and being honorable and having integrity with those for whom we have responsibility — everyone's quality of life goes up.

The fourth side of the family square has to do with building a holy home built on the foundation of honor and respect. Building a holy home has to do with all the other three sides of the square called family. Respect for parents and all in authority over us; being honorable to those for whom we have responsibility and having a high quality family life are all involved with building a holy home.

In contrast to a holy home, for many people today, the home is little more than a large telephone booth where arrangements are made to leave.

A Large Telephone Booth
Where Arrangements Are Made To Leave

Think about it. The family and the home are in serious trouble today because everyone is on the go, usually in different directions. Everyone seems to be caught in the chaos of busyness, obligations, sports, television, noise, jobs, long hours away from the family, and the demands made on us by others. In other words, the modern home all too often is a place which we constantly leave. A phone call is made or the phone rings and off people go. The holy home is built on honor and respect. That means we take time together, time to communicate, time to listen, time to pray. The biblical corrective for the alluring, attractive distractions of life today is taking the initiative and providing quality time for family members.

Winston Churchill once remarked, "Some people make things happen. They are the achievers. Some people watch things happen. They are the professional critics. And some people don't know things happen. They are the sleepers." Today, some people seem to be asleep in relationship to the breakdown of the home. They just don't see what is happening. Others are critical of what is happening, but do little or nothing to change it. Still, others make a difference by taking the initiative and trying to restore the home to the place it was given by God. This chapter is intended as an encouragement to those who not only see the problem and criticize what is happening to the family, but seek to make a difference by their actions.

How could people be sleepers when it seems so apparent that serious damage is being done daily to the institution of family and the Christian home? Over half of American marriages today end in divorce. Single family homes are on a radical increase. Homes with the only parent working, trying to make ends meet, with the children left to others to raise, are on the rise. Second, third, and fourth marriages leave children in the wilderness wondering who they are, whose they are, and what they are supposed to do. Many parents are going in so many directions that little time is spent on the nurturing and care of the children. Ethical relativism is taught in our schools and our society. The lack of belief in ethical absolutes causes chaos everywhere. How could anyone be asleep through all this chaos? Chaos is catching. Do we have to succumb?

The launching pad for taking action to restore the family to a central place in life and to make holy homes is the restoration of honor and respect. Critical analysis is not enough. If many modern homes are little more than large telephone booths where arrangements are made to leave, isn't there something that we can do about it? Can't we find some ways to turn these large telephone booths into holy homes? Can't we do more than analyze what is wrong? The Fourth Commandment gives us a launching pad to take the initiative against the destruction of home life and the activism that is all too typical of modern life.

Honor and respect. We need not only stand *against* the immorality of our times which is ruining our lives. We need to stand *for* something — honor and respect for God and one another. Is it possible to recover a reverence for the home and family? Yes, I believe it is. It isn't easy, but it isn't impossible. We may never get to the promised land on this one, but that is no excuse for not taking the initiative in the right direction. We don't have to stay in bondage. We can start the journey, the end of which we may not fully know until we die and see our Father in our heavenly home.

Let's look at the functions of the family and consider some practical ways to make our homes holy.

The Functions Of The Family

Dolores Curran, a Roman Catholic author, columnist, and family consultant, says that there are five traditional functions of the family. Consider economic, protective, religious, educational, and status-conferring factors as you think about the ways in which you and your family might take the initiative against what is happening to the family today and try to build a holy home on the solid foundation of honor and respect.

1. Economic. Traditionally in our society, the man was the breadwinner and the woman the homemaker. Today, those roles have broken down. Often both husband and wife work. Often the responsibilities of home and children are neglected. Sometimes the new pattern of both parents working is necessary because the family cannot survive on one income. Single moms (or single dads) have to work to put bread on the table. They must use a day care center.

But, sometimes both husband and wife work outside the home because the couple wants luxuries that cannot be otherwise purchased. In this latter situation, shouldn't a re-evaluation of priorities be made so that one or the other of the parents stays home to provide more quality time with small children?

My daughter, Mary Cousler, is writing a book titled, *Mommyhood*.

In that book she tells of the time when in order to make ends meet, she and her husband were both working. They had their son in a day care center. When Mary went to pick up her son one day, she was shocked to see that he was more attached to the day care provider than to her. There and then, Mary and her husband decided that something had to change.

Today, Mary is a stay-at-home mom. She has three sons. Her husband works three jobs to help pay the bills. That is not a perfect solution, but it is better in their minds than both parents working and the three children being raised by someone else.

In her book, Mary urges support for the stay-at-home moms who are fighting an uphill battle in today's society to provide a holy home for their spouses and children. She says that she is not putting down working mothers, but that stay-at-home-moms need encouragement.

One parent staying home is not an option in all situations. One parent staying home is certainly not the only way to rebuild respect and honor for parents and the home, but isn't stay-at-home motherhood (or fatherhood) a neglected option which more Christian couples should consider today?

In addition to the economic factor, consider the protective, religious, educational, and status-conferring factors in building a holy home.

2. Protective. Traditionally, the family has been a place of safety from our enemies and a place to find solace for our

souls. Don't children need a sense of security and safety today? Doesn't a holy home mean that the home is a shelter for those who live in it? When children are protected by love and discipline, aren't they more likely to honor and respect their parents?

3. Religious. Children need to be taught that their home is a church and their church is a home. Part of the initiative against the oppressive forces that are destroying the home today is for the partnership of these two great institutions: the home and the church. We need to pass on the stories of our faith and what God has done in history to our children. A holy home and a church that cares about the family both focus on Bible stories. Storytelling at home around shared meals and at bedtime are parts of a plan to build a holy home in which there is respect and honor for all family members.

4. Educational. Passing on the truths of the past from one generation to the next and teaching children how to think is not only the function of the school, but the home. Passing on a Christian world-view takes time, but is well worth the effort, especially when there are such diverse and disruptive philosophies of the secular world.

5. Status-conferring. In a holy home where honor and respect are more than words, children gain self-esteem and confidence for living. By observing honor and respect in the words and deeds of parents, character is built. By observing honor and respect shown to God, other family members and those outside the family, children learn to imitate that kind of honor and respect.

No easy answers please, but aren't these five factors needed to examine the biblical admonition to show honor and respect to those over us in the Lord? There is no panacea for what is wrong with families today, but we need to take the initiative in these areas, not just react to what society dictates. Different Christian families will find different ways to answer the questions raised in these and other areas. But, aren't all Christians called to look carefully at values in these categories in the light of the Fourth Commandment which calls for honor and respect for God and parents and home?

To take the initiative against the potential destruction of the family today, Christians need to do more than complain. They need to be encouraged not to quit the uphill battle to restore honor and respect to the home.

I am reminded of a Catholic nun who entered a convent of a special order where she took a vow of silence. Every ten years she had the opportunity to say something to the Mother Superior about her experience of the last ten years. She was confined to using only two words when she spoke. After the first ten years, Mother Superior called her into the office and said, "Sister, you have been with us for ten years. You can break your vow of silence and say two words."

"Work's hard," said the nun. Then she went back to her job.

Ten years passed. Again, Mother Superior said, "You have been with us twenty years. This is your second opportunity to say two words."

"Food's bad," said the nun. Then she returned to her duties.

Ten years later Mother Superior called her in again. "Since you have been with us thirty years, you may speak two more words."

"I quit," said the nun.

"That doesn't surprise me a bit," replied Mother Superior. "All you've done for thirty years is complain."

When it comes to the modern family, the work is hard, the food is not always the most expensive kind, and at times we feel like we want to quit. This chapter is intended as an encouragement not to quit.

You don't have to agree with the practical suggestions in this chapter, but you are urged to keep the words "honor" and "respect" in your mind daily and find ways to build a holy home whether your family is the traditional husband, wife, and two children, you are a widow or a widower, or you are a single or divorced mom or dad struggling against great odds in a crooked and perverse world. As Peter said on Pentecost, "Save yourselves from this corrupt generation" (Acts 2:40). Let me add, "Save your family from this crooked generation, too."

The Fourth Commandment is a prohibition against making the home and the family a part of the crooked generation in which we live, but it is also an invitation to build a Christian home on biblical values that work.

Let me put all that I have tried to say another way. When all else fails, why not go back to the directions? The directions for a well-lived life are in the Bible. The directions for a holy home are in the Fourth Commandment. The summary of these directions is to show honor and respect for the family.

Questions For Your Personal Consideration And/Or Group Discussion

1. Read Proverbs 22:6. How does this apply today?

2. Read Ephesians 6:1-4. What application does this passage have?

3. If a visitor from Mars said to you, "Take me to your leader," to whom would you go?

4. Discuss this quotation: "The day a child realizes that all adults are imperfect, he becomes an adolescent. The day he forgives them, he becomes an adult. The day he forgives himself, he becomes wise."

5. Which of these are needed for a holy home?
   ___ a Christ-like climate
   ___ the fragrance of love
   ___ the feel of faith
   ___ the example of selfless good deeds done by parents
   ___ honor and respect
   ___ a sense of safety and caring
   ___ the example of understanding and gratitude

6. Discuss Proverbs 13:24.
   What is good about discipline?
   What is going too far?

7. Read Acts 4:18-20 and discuss this passage in the light of the Fourth Commandment.

Digging Deeper

1. Read Deuteronomy 6:6-9. What needs to be taught to children to give them a sense of God?

2. Read Deuteronomy 6:13-15. What difference does it make what God we worship?

3. Read Psalm 78:5-7. What should we do for the next generation?

4. What difference does expressed gratitude make for children who observe it between parents and hear it from parents?

5. Turning away from griping and toward gratitude in the family is one of the most important ways to make a holy home. For help in this area, see my book, *Turning Griping Into Gratitude* (CSS Publishing Company, Lima, Ohio, 2000). It is a book on Psalms with discussion questions at the end of each chapter that can be used in families, in groups, or in classes to help people to advance in their communication of gratitude to God and one another.

6. Steve Allen, the comedian, was the chairman of the Parents Television Council. In his book, *Vulgarians At The Gate* (Prometheus Books, 2001), Allen says,

> *The coarsening of our entire culture is by no means a simple matter. But oppose it we must, for the consequences or rearing millions of initially innocent children in a social atmosphere characterized by vulgarity, violence, brutish manners, the collapse of the family, and general disrespect for traditional codes of conduct is to chill the blood of even the most tolerant observers.*

7. We may never get to the promised land in making our homes into holy places, but that is no excuse not to start the journey.

Chapter Five

Prohibitions And Invitations In The Fifth Commandment

You shall not murder.   — Exodus 20:13

You have heard that it was said to the people long ago, "Do not murder, and anyone who murders will be subject to judgment." But I tell you that anyone who is angry with his brother will be subject to judgment. Again, anyone who says to his brother, "Raca," is answerable to the Sanhedrin. But anyone who says, "You fool," will be in danger of the fire of hell.
       — Matthew 5:21-22

The Fifth Commandment speaks against murder. Jesus' interpretation of this Commandment has to do with anger. When looking at the Old Testament passage, we might exclaim, "Me, a murderer? Don't be silly. I'm against taking the life of another person. People who murder others should be locked up and the key thrown away, or they should face capital punishment for their dastardly deeds." When we look at Jesus' words in the Sermon on the Mount, we can confess, "Me, a murderer! God forgive me for my sins."

This Commandment relates to hot topics like anger, war, capital punishment, suicide, active euthanasia, and abortion. These topics are discussed at the end of this chapter (Questions and Digging Deeper). Here we focus on Jesus' words about anger and murder.

Murder means the intentional destruction of another human being. A concrete example might help. Jay Dull is a murderer. He murdered a taxi-cab driver in Muncie, Indiana, in 1960, during an armed robbery. The cab driver lunged for the gun Jay was holding. Jay backed off and then hit the cab driver with the butt of the shotgun.

At his trial, against the advice of his lawyer, Jay took the stand to try to explain his side of what happened. The prosecuting attorney attacked him. Jay got defensive. The attack continued. Emotions rose. The prosecutor asked Jay directly if he was sorry for what he had done. Defiantly, Jay replied, "Hell, no. I'd do it again if I had the chance."

Jay Dull, the defiant murderer, was assigned to the electric chair. Head shaven, leg shaven, and last meal ordered, Jay came within twelve hours of being electrocuted. He got clemency from the governor of Indiana. He went back to death row. Later he was transferred to the jail in Muncie, Indiana, because he sought a hearing from the judge on a plea of incompetent counsel. As the pastor of the local Lutheran church in Muncie, I was asked to visit Jay.

Jay told me that he was guilty of murder, but that he had finally seen the need for God in his life. He knew that he deserved to be punished, but he hoped that he could pay for his crime with a life sentence in prison.

Jay Dull, the defiant murderer became Jay Dull, a repentant Christian. In 1965, I confirmed Jay in the Muncie jail with the church council of Holy Trinity Lutheran Church present. Jay Dull broke the Fifth Commandment by taking the life of another person. I mention his story for two reasons. First, he is a clear example of what it means to break the Fifth Commandment. Second, his motivation for the killing was anger. When the cab driver lunged for the gun, Jay's stored up anger and hatred exploded.

Unlike Jay, most of us have never murdered another human being. Like Jay, all of us have known those times when stored up anger has exploded in actions which were not our proudest moments. In the passage in Matthew, Jesus is talking about the danger of stored up anger. The Bible says, "Anyone who hates his brother is a murderer" (1 John 3:15).

The Dangers Of Stored-up Anger

In his commentary on the Gospel of Matthew, William Barclay gives us insight into the meaning of Jesus' words. The Greek verb used in Matthew 5:21-22 which we translate "anger" comes from the root word *orge*. In Greek there are two words for anger. The second is *thumos*, which is like a flame which comes from dried straw. It quickly blazes up and just as quickly dies. While *thumos* anger can be dangerous, it is a natural reaction which is sometimes appropriate and sometimes not, but is always short-lived. The anger that Jesus condemns is *orge*, anger which is stored up and nursed over a period of time. The New International Bible translation of Matthew 5:22 is "Any one who nurses anger against his brother must be brought to judgment." Nursing anger is very dangerous.

Nursing anger means holding on to resentments. Resentment eventually, if not immediately, results in revenge. Revenge is a deadly sin. The Bible says, "In your anger do not sin. Do not let the sun go down while you are still angry" (Ephesians 4:26).

Some people are more controlled than others. Some express anger often; some less frequently. But all human beings at times go out of control with what the ancients called "temporary insanity." As Jesus described it, we have all broken the Fifth Commandment and are subject to judgment.

Jesus brings the danger of *orge* anger to our attention, not to condemn us, but to help us see the need for repentance and new life. No matter how hard we try, we will from time to time fly off the handle at someone, but with the proper focus and help from God we can avoid the pitfalls related to nursing anger, even when from a human point of view we have a right to it. We have little or no control over what people do to us, but we can exercise control over how we respond to what people do to us. That's why Jesus said,

> *You have heard that it was said, "Love you neighbor and hate your enemy." But I tell you: Love your enemies and pray for those who persecute you, that you may be sons of your Father in heaven. He causes his*

sun to rise on the evil and the good, and sends rain on the righteous and the unrighteous. If you love those who love you, what reward will you get? Are not even the tax collectors doing that? And if you greet only your brothers, what are you doing more than others? Do not even pagans do that? Be perfect, therefore, as your heavenly Father is perfect. — Matthew 5:43-46

The word we translate "perfect" in Greek is *telos*. *Telos* does not mean "without error"; it means "whole." In other words, Jesus is saying if you want to love your enemies as God loves his enemies, you must be whole, like God, not divided by anger which has been nursed until it has gained control over your actions. Resentment is like taking poison in the hope that this will somehow hurt someone who hurt you. Resentment is a growing cancer in the soul. If you catch it early and submit it to the Divine Physician, *orge* anger need not destroy you, but if you neglect to do anything about it, it will kill you.

Unrighteous Anger And Righteous Anger

Making the distinction between *orge* anger and *thumos* anger is important for our consideration of the Fifth Commandment. Making the distinction between righteous anger and unrighteous anger is equally important. Jesus was angry when he found money changers in the temple turning his Father's house into a den of thieves. That was righteous anger. Like Jesus, Christians have used righteous anger to make needed social change like doing away with slavery, seeking civil rights, and fighting prejudice on all fronts. *Righteous anger is like a pure burning fire. Unrighteous anger is like baking the garbage in your stove.*

Internalized, unrighteous anger is the theme of Jesus' words about the Fifth Commandment. Internalized, unrighteous anger is what lies behind much of the conflict in our lives. Many people experience this kind of anger in their marriages. At her fiftieth wedding anniversary, a woman was asked, "Have you ever considered divorce?" "Never," she replied. "Murder, yes; divorce, no."

Internalized, unrighteous anger often lies behind health problems. Dr. Granger Westberg, a Lutheran pastor who spent much of his career working in medical schools, asked a group of doctors, nurses, and pastors a question. "There is one thing which medical research shows lies behind much sickness," he said. "What is it?" The audience guessed stress, smoking, drinking, and conflict. "Those are all problems," Westberg said, "but the one factor that recent research has shown presents the greatest danger to our health is revenge."

Revenge comes from resentment. Resentment is internalized anger. Internalized, unrighteous anger is not only dangerous for those who are on the receiving side of it; it is equally dangerous for those who are controlled by it. In over forty years of ministry, I have started over 500 koinonia (fellowship) groups in five churches and many conferences. One of the questions we ask people in these groups to answer on unsigned cards is, "What is your greatest problem as a Christian?" The most frequent answer is "anger." The same emotion that was at work in Jay Dull, the murderer, is at work in all of us.

Isn't there something we can do about this pervasive problem? Yes, I believe there is.

The Expulsive Power Of Gratitude And Love

Dr. Westberg, mentioned earlier, said to his audience, "There is one thing recent research has shown to help control revenge, resentment, and anger. In addition, this one thing is more conducive to physical, mental, and spiritual health than any other factor. After many wrong guesses by the pastors, doctors, and nurses, Dr. Westberg said, "The one thing that brings health more than any other is gratitude. The right attitude is gratitude."

The attitude of gratitude to God is an act of love for God. God first loved us by creating us and sending Jesus as our Savior. Gratitude for that love is the first step toward health. Expressing gratitude to God through private and corporate worship and prayer is a step in the direction of seeing anger for what it is and taking the initiative against it. Many hymns and spiritual songs are expressions of gratitude. Singing to God is a sign of gratitude; it is a good health practice. As one church put it, "Join our choir; sing praises to God and get healthy."

A second step toward better health by overcoming *orge* anger is to love our neighbors and our enemies as God has loved us. "Love your enemies and pray for those who persecute you," Jesus said (Matthew 5:44). Nursing anger divides. Love, even for those who do not love us, makes us whole, like our heavenly Father. One of the reasons Jesus warns us about the dangers of internalized, unrighteous anger and invites us into the world of loving our enemies is that he wants us to be healthy, not sick.

Jesus condemns selfish anger, anger that broods, and anger that insults or seeks revenge against the neighbor. Thus he clears the way for the expulsive power of the new affection called selfless love. Jesus wants to work the righteousness of God in every heart. The Bible says, "The anger of man does not work the righteousness of God" (James 1:20).

Saint Paul, the apostle, speaks of genuine love of those who hurt us.

> *Love must be sincere. Hate what is evil; cling to what is good. Be devoted to one another in brotherly love. Honor one another above yourselves. Never be lacking in zeal, but keep your spiritual fervor, serving the Lord. Be joyful in hope, patient in affliction, faithful in prayer. Share with God's people who are in need. Practice hospitality.* — Romans 12:9-13

Sincere social ministry and selfless hospitality for those in need are expressions of the expulsive power of a new affection.

Saint Paul goes on to explain the specifics of loving our enemies as an option to anger that leads to revenge.

> *Bless those who persecute you; bless and do not curse. Rejoice with those who rejoice; mourn with those who mourn. Live in harmony with one another. Do not be proud, but be willing to associate with people of low position. Do not be conceited.*
>
> *Do not repay anyone evil for evil. Be careful to do what is right in the eyes of everybody. If it is possible, as far as it depends on you, live at peace with everyone. Do not take revenge, my friends, but leave room*

> *for God's wrath, for it is written: "It is mine to avenge; I will repay," says the Lord. On the contrary:*
>   *"If your enemy is hungry, feed him; if he is thirsty, give him something to drink. In doing this, you will heap burning coals on his head."*
>   *Do not be overcome by evil, but overcome evil with good.* — Romans 12:14-21

In other words, there is no need to repay those who hurt us. Instead, we can leave it in the hands of God who sees all sides of what happens to us and is the only one who can judge rightly. Instead of getting caught in the trap of reciprocity which then goes on and on, we can take the initiative by loving our enemies.

Martin Luther says that the meaning of the Fifth Commandment is that we should help and befriend our neighbor in every need, even if he or she has hurt us. Tolerance of those who do us no harm is easy. Proactive love for those who don't deserve it is quite another thing.

George Forell, a professor of ethics at the University of Iowa School of Religion for many years, says that we cannot achieve this kind of love by our own power.

> *The crux of the Christian fulfillment of the Fifth Commandment is its application to those who are our enemies.... Out of our own power we can love the good, the beautiful, the lovable, but it is only through the power of faith in Christ that we can love those who hate us and who are, humanly speaking, utterly unlovable.*

The Fifth Commandment is a call to see other people the way Christ sees them, with less judgment and more love. The Fifth Commandment throws us onto the only hope we have of salvation: the grace of God in Christ. The Fifth Commandment not only calls us to confess, "Me, a murderer!" but in addition to depends on the biblical promise that while God hates sin, God loves the sinner. And God loves repentance.

It isn't easy to admit that we are sinners. It is the hardest thing of all, but the one thing needful. Even old time Christians struggle with recognition of sin and repentance in thoughts, words, and deeds. After hearing a sermon on the Fifth Commandment in which the pastor said that each of us is hopelessly embroiled in internalized, unrighteous anger, a little old lady confronted the pastor at the church door with this remark: "Well, if we are that bad, God help us."

"Precisely," said the pastor. "That is what Christianity is all about."

Questions For Your Personal Consideration And/Or Group Discussion

1. Read Genesis 4:2-9. In the story of Cain and Abel, the question is raised, "Am I my brother's keeper?" How do you answer that question?

2. How does road rage relate to Jesus' interpretation of the Fifth Commandment?

3. Read the Digging Deeper section on the following pages. Remembering that Christians take different positions on the controversial social application of the Fifth Commandment and Jesus' interpretation of it, consider the following topics:
   a. War
   b. Capital punishment
   c. Suicide
   d. Euthanasia
   e. Abortion

4. Discuss this quote: "Resentment is like taking poison in the hope that it will hurt someone who hurt you."

Digging Deeper

1. War involves killing other human beings. It is generally not considered to be murder, but some Christians are pacifists; they refuse to go to war.

2. Capital punishment involves killing another human being. The Bible can be quoted on both sides of this issue. Some of the pros and cons of capital punishment are listed below:

   ### For
   - Capital punishment is appropriate because the state treats killers like they have treated others (an eye for an eye).
   - Capital punishment relieves the public of major expenses related to long incarceration.
   - It relieves the resentment and pressure on the family of the victim.
   - It permanently keeps the murderer from repeating the crime.
   - It serves to deter those who are tempted to kill others.
   - It helps to avoid private retribution.

   ### Against
   - Capital punishment is inappropriate because Jesus teaches us an ethic beyond the eye for an eye theory of the Old Testament.
   - Capital punishment results in great expenses beyond incarceration because of lawyers' fees, judges' salaries, and the amount of money it takes to process the various petitions of those on death row.
   - It may relieve the family of victims by giving them a sense of revenge, but is revenge the proper motivation for Christians?
   - While it permanently keeps the murderer from repeating the crime, so does permanent incarceration.

- Case studies show that the states with the highest capital punishment rate are also the states with the highest rate of murders.
- Granted, it helps to avoid private retribution, but incarceration does that, too.
- It is morally wrong to kill people for killing people.
- It is cruel and inhumane punishment.
- Human error can mean that people who are put to death are innocent.
- **Case studies show that for those who have capital, there seldom is capital punishment.** In other words, it is mostly minorities and poor people who actually are killed for killing other people. Capital punishment is not evenly administered.

3. There are two kinds of suicide. The first might be called "despondent suicide," the second "deliberate, defiant suicide." When a person is despondent and depressed, he or she may not see any way out of a dilemma which confronts them. Christians should work with such people to help them see that God never deserts them. See John 14:18.

   On the other hand, deliberate, defiant suicide is the action of a person who does not believe in God and is involved in what the New Testament calls "blasphemy against the Holy Spirit." The work of the Holy Spirit is to bring us to repentance and faith in Christ. Blasphemy of the Holy Spirit is the unforgivable sin.

   No repentance is possible if we refuse to see our sin and/or refuse to bring that sin to God. Forgiveness has been accomplished by Christ on the cross, but repentance and faith in Christ are the way we personally appropriate what has been accomplished. See Matthew 12:31-32. Only God can judge the eternal state of a person who commits suicide.

4. Active euthanasia, however noble the motive, cannot be condoned, even if intended solely for the purpose of ending the suffering of a patient or loved one. No one should play God. Assisted suicide statutes like the one in Oregon called "Death With Dignity" is contrary to the traditions and teachings of Judaism and Christianity. According to the *Los Angeles Times* (June 6, 1998) the Oregon law allows a patient who has been diagnosed by two doctors as having less than six months to live to seek a doctor's prescription for a lethal dose of barbiturates. The patient must be determined to be of "right mind."

   Passive euthanasia means not taking heroic measures to save one's own life or that of a loved one. Many Christians have living wills that tell doctors not to take heroic measures to save their lives if their sickness will inevitably lead to death in the immediate future.

   Sometimes the lines between active and passive euthanasia are blurred. Medical advances continue to challenge the distinction between what we can do and what we should do in this difficult area, but we must not bypass consideration of Christian ethics in the decisions we make.

5. Abortion means taking the life of an unborn child. The "pro-life" and "pro-choice" debate goes on. Ethical, medical, and legal questions about when life begins is at the heart of this question. The question of the rights of the mother and the child are also involved. Adoption is a good option to abortion in most cases.

   Some Christians take the position that if rape or incest is involved in the pregnancy, abortion may be the best of several bad choices. For some people, choosing abortion is also the best of several bad alternatives if the life of the mother is in danger while she is giving birth. In these circumstances, the choice may not be between right and wrong, but between all bad choices. In these cases, we sometimes must choose the best of several bad options. We are called to be repentant when we must choose between several bad choices.

Chapter Six

Prohibitions And Invitations In The Sixth Commandment

You shall not commit adultery. — Exodus 20:14

You have heard that it was said, "Do not commit adultery." But I tell you that anyone who looks at a woman lustfully has already committed adultery with her in his heart. — Matthew 5:27-28

There are many misunderstandings of adultery in our society. A little girl once asked her Sunday school teacher, "Do adults have as much fun in adultery as children do in childhood?" No, little girl, they don't. She misunderstood the meaning of adultery. Another child said, "The Sixth Commandment is 'Thou shalt not *admit* adultery.'"

In our day, many do not *admit* adultery. They think this Commandment no longer applies; anything goes between consenting adults. According to what is sometimes called "the new morality" in the area of sex, people can do whatever pleases them as long as they both agree to the act. According to ethical relativism, private sexual behavior is only the business of the people involved. This is not a new morality. It has been around as long as there have been people. Adultery is just as self-defeating today as it was when God gave the Sixth Commandment to Moses on Mount Sinai. It is

85

easy to forget that those who break God's Commandments are broken by God's Commandments.

Adultery is generally defined as sexual intercourse by a married person with someone other than his/her spouse, thus violating the marriage bed. The trouble with that definition is that it limits adultery to married people. Jesus widens the definition so that it not only includes infidelity by marriage partners, but lust as well.

Jesus speaks of adultery in terms of the heart. If you lust after a woman in your heart, he says that, too, is adultery. Jesus widens the approach to adultery (see Digging Deeper) to include lustful thoughts, premarital sexual acts, and extramarital sexual relations. In John 4:1-42, Jesus deals with a woman who had had five husbands and was then living with a man who was not her husband (John 4:17-18). Jesus offered her forgiveness which she accepted, but it is clear in the story that he does not accept cohabitation without the benefit of marriage.

Sexual sins, like all other sins, can be forgiven, but first we must see that what we have done is wrong and repent before God. That's where today's ethical relativism puts many people in serious danger. If you think that God's Sixth Commandment is just one opinion among many opinions, you will not *admit* your sin. You won't repent. But whether we like it or not, sexual intercourse, outside the fence God has placed around sex, is sin.

Prohibitions: God Has Placed A Fence Around Sex

God has placed a fence around sex. Within the fence of love, marriage, and fidelity, sex is not only a good thing, but a wonder-filled way to participate in the creation of a child with little eyes, ears, fingers, and toes. Within the fence of love and marriage, sex is a wonderful way to fulfill our physical and spiritual needs to intimately *know* another person.

In the Bible, to *know* another person means to have intimacy with them. In Genesis 4:1 we read that Adam *knew* his wife Eve. That means that they had intimate sexual relations. It was more than physical intimacy; it was spiritual intimacy as well. It is not by accident that the Bible urges us to *know* God. To *know* God means to have a spiritual, intimate relationship with him. Psalm 46:10 puts it this way: "Be still and *know* that I am God" (RSV — emphasis mine).

Outside the fence that God places around sex, it becomes a destructive force to ourselves and others. Sex outside of marriage had caused untold misery for thousands upon thousands of people. Doesn't God know what he is doing when he puts sex inside the fence of love and marriage?

If a young woman has a beautiful prom dress, she wouldn't throw it in the mud and jump up and down on it, would she? If a young man went on an adventure and discovered a large and valuable gold nugget, he wouldn't make a common door knob out of it, would he? Neither does God intend for us to use our gift of sexuality in a dirty or common way. Sexuality is intended for two special, godly purposes — first, to enjoy your spouse physically and spiritually; and second to produce children.

Some years ago, Dr. Edgar Carlson, then president of Gustavus Adolphus College, told a chapel gathering of college students about the meaning of the Sixth Commandment. He said,

> *Of course you can take the most precious things and make them cheap, if you want to. You can take the royal velvet of a king's robe and make carpet rags out of it, but who would? You can take a diamond-studded bracelet, and make a drawer pull for the kitchen sink out of it, if you want to, but who would? You can take a million dollar bond and buy a dollar watch with it, but who would do that except a fool who doesn't know the value of things? And you can take this intimate, personal and dedicated thing called sexuality which holds out the promise of being one of God's richest gifts to you and cash it in for a moment's sensual gratification, but who would be such a fool?*

Inside the fence of love, marriage, and fidelity, sexual expression is a precious gift of God for a husband and wife to enjoy and use creatively. Outside the fence of love, marriage, and fidelity, the precious treasure turns into something ugly. Inside the fence, sex between husband and wife is holy; it is the fulfillment of the marriage vows to love and cherish. Outside this fence sex is unholy. Consider the diagram below. God is at the apex; the husband and wife at the other points in the triangular fence.

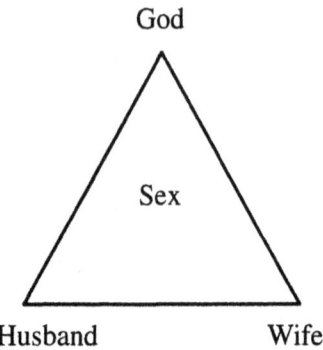

Extramarital and premarital sexual intercourse are outside the fence of honor for God and love and fidelity in marriage. God, who made us, knows what is best for us. Out of love, a wise mother tells her children not to put their fingers into the fire on the top of the stove. Out of love, a wise father tells his children not to run out in front of traffic on a super-highway. In like manner, out of love God tells his children not to take sexual intercourse outside the marriage relationship or they will get hurt. God knows better than we do what is best for us.

Non-marital sexual intercourse is outside the fence God has erected to protect us. So is lust.

Me, An Adulterer?

Some years ago I tried to teach a group of confirmation students that there is a difference between temptation and sin. I also tried to teach them that sex is a good thing, not a bad thing. I told them, "If you look at a pretty girl and admire her, that's not a sin."

"Wow," said a thirteen-year-old boy. "I didn't know that it was okay to look at a girl like that."

"But if you look too long, that is a sin," I quickly added.

"How long is too long?" he asked.

We don't know how long is too long, but we know you can look too long and that looking too long is lust. Martin Luther put it this way, "You cannot keep the birds of temptation from flying over your head, but you can keep them from building a nest in your mind." In the area of sex, the birds of temptation all too often build their nests in our minds.

Jesus teaches that it is possible to lust after another person and thus commit adultery in the heart. In this way we are all adulterers. An adulteress was brought to Jesus by self-righteous sinners who were trying to trap him. These self-righteous men thought they had set the perfect trap. "What should we do with her?" they asked. According to the Law of Moses, she should be stoned to death. Jesus had a reputation for compassion and mercy. What would he do? If he said, "Set her free," his enemies would say, "He places himself above the Law of Moses." If he said, "Stone her," they would point out that he was a hypocrite for not showing mercy. A perfect trap.

Drawing with a stick in the sand, Jesus meditated for a few moments. Then he replied, "Let him who is without sin cast the first stone." People quietly dropped their stones and left. Jesus and the woman were left alone. The woman trembled. "Has no one condemned you?" Jesus asked.

"No one, Lord," she replied.

"Neither do I condemn you. Go and sin no more."

Note three things in the story. First, sexual sins can be forgiven. The woman was freed from her sins. Some people carry their sexual sins on their backs all their lives, not acknowledging that they can be relieved by a simple, but sincere act of contrition.

Second, Jesus said that the woman should not continue in her sinful ways. It is as if he is telling her, "Don't put your hand in the fire or you will get burned. Don't run out on the road and stand there or you will get hurt."

Third, Jesus challenged those who condemned the woman. They, too, were sinful. Jesus knew that they were filled with lust. Casting stones in a self-righteous way is out of line because all of us can get caught in the web of lust. Some get caught in this web less frequently; some more frequently, but God knows all of our thoughts, both good and bad.

Whatever gets your attention, gets you. If you give your attention to sex in a distorted way, sex will turn on you and gain control over you. With the movies, magazines, and books of our time filled with pictures and stories of distorted sexuality, it is hard not to get caught in the trap. That is why we need to focus on the Lord first in our lives.

> *Unless that which is above you*
> *Controls that which is within you,*
> *That which is around you*
> *Will.*
>
> — Anonymous

The moral decay, ethical relativism, and permissiveness that fill our society present major challenges to all of us, especially youth who are looking for guidance and often not finding it in adults who do not *admit* their sinfulness.

A teenager sent me this anonymous poem:

Delinquent?

We read in the papers and hear on the air
Of killings and stealing and crime everywhere.
We sigh and we say as we notice the trend
"Are they all rebels, have they no end?"

But can we be sure it's their fault alone?
Maybe a part of it is also our own.
Are we the guilty who place in their way
Too many things that lead them astray?

Too much money to spend. Too much idle time?
Too many movies of passion and crime,
Too many children encouraged to roam,
By too many parents who won't stay at home.

Kids don't make the movies. They don't write the books.
They don't paint the pictures of gangsters and crooks.
They don't write magazines. They don't run the bars.
They don't make the liquor. They don't make the cars.

They don't peddle drugs that addle the brain.
That's all done by older folks greedy for gain.
By the law of the blameless the Savior made known
"Who's there among us to cast the first stone?"

For in so many cases it's sad, but true.
The title "delinquent" fits older folks, too.
— Anonymous

We all are guilty of breaking the Sixth Commandment in our thoughts and by not showing the best examples of fidelity to the younger generation, but aren't there some positive things we can do to combat the sexual revolution all around us today? We can ask forgiveness for inappropriate deeds and thoughts. We can also seek to rebuild the Christian home today on the values of the Bible and prayerful, common-sense approaches to our spouses.

Invitations: Building Affair-proof Marriages

While there is no way to assure that a sexual affair will not happen in your family, there are some things that can be done to take the initiative against the sexual revolution that threatens family life today. In his book, *His Needs, Her Needs*,[11] Willard F. Harley, Jr., a clinical psychologist, lists ways in which a husband should try to meet the needs of his wife and a wife should try to meet the needs of her husband. The first thing to do is identify these needs. Gary and Barbara Rosberg have a different list.[12] Whether you agree or disagree with Harley or the Rosbergs, consider their lists as a starting point for conversations about this important subject.

His Needs

Harley	Gary and Barbara Rosberg
1. Sexual fulfillment	1. Unconditional love and acceptance
2. Recreational companionship	2. Sexual intimacy

3. An attractive spouse
4. Domestic support
5. Admiration

3. Companionship
4. Encouragement and affirmation
5. Spiritual intimacy

Her Needs
1. Affection
2. Conversation
3. Honesty and openness
4. Financial support
5. Family commitment

1. Unconditional love and acceptance
2. Emotional intimacy
3. Spiritual intimacy
4. Encouragement and affirmation
5. Companionship

    Too many men think that women think like men think; too many women think that men think like women think. The lists provide a starting point for discussion between husbands and wives. Instead of trying to change one another, why not try to meet the needs of your spouse, before thinking of yourself? Dr. Harley says, "While most people would deny they could ever get involved in an affair, the hard truth is that, under the right (or wrong) conditions, any of us can fall victim, if our basic needs are not being met."

Questions For Your Personal Consideration And/Or Group Discussion

1. What do you think about the fence of love, marriage, and fidelity that this chapter says God has placed around sex?

2. Consider the statement, "Whatever gets your attention, gets you. Sex is a strong drive which easily gets our attention and can get us into trouble."

3. Do you agree or disagree with the anonymous poem "Delinquent" in this chapter?

4. Study the two lists of His Needs and Her Needs provided in this chapter. If you are in a group, you may want to follow the following suggestions. First, divide the group into men and women; then into smaller groups of four people in each gender group. Second, in each group of four women or four men have each person in each group write down what they think the needs of their own gender are, using the lists provided in this chapter. Third, have each group revise the list for their gender as they see fit. Fourth, have each small group of four discuss what they have written. Fifth, bring the whole group together for discussion.

5. In a fifth-grade Sunday school class a little girl was asked about Lot's wife. She replied, "Lot's wife was a pillar of fire by day and a ball of fire by night." Discuss.

6. Another child said, "A Christian should have only one wife. This is called monotony." Discuss.

7. All of the Commandments are given to protect something. The Sixth Commandment was given to protect _____ _____. (fill in the blank)

8. Consider the purpose of sex in marriage. Check the answers below you consider correct and add any additional answers you have.
   a. Procreation
   b. Enjoyment
   c. An expression of love as unity and intimacy, both physical and spiritual
   d. _____
   e. _____

9. Seen on a billboard:
   > JUST WHAT IS IT THAT YOU DON'T UNDERSTAND ABOUT THESE WORDS, "THOU SHALT NOT"?
   > — GOD

Digging Deeper

1. When it comes to sexual sins, people often look for loopholes. Mel Kieschnick, who wrote the Introduction for this book, tells the story of W. C. Fields. When hospitalized, Fields, not a "churchgoer," was found reading the Bible. His friend said, "I didn't know you were so religious." "I'm not," Fields replied, "just looking for loopholes."

2. Consider taking a group of people from an adult education class, a new members class or a fellowship group, or Bible study group on retreat to discuss the book *His Needs, Her Needs* by Willard F. Harley or *The Five Needs Of Men And Women* by Gary and Barbara Rosberg.

3. Do you agree or disagree with Harley who says, "Once a spouse lacks fulfillment of any of the five needs, it creates a thirst that must be quenched. If changes do not take place within the marriage to care for that need, the individual will face the powerful temptation to fill it outside of marriage."

4. Do you agree with Martin Luther's distinction between temptation and sin using the birds of temptation as an example?

5. Has your church ever sponsored a marriage enrichment or marriage encounter retreat for couples? If not, would it help the couples in your church to go on such a retreat?

6. Consider the following definition of adultery:

In a special sense, sexual intercourse of a married man with a female not his wife, or that of a married woman with a man not her husband. Under Mosaic Law, adultery was punished with death (Leviticus 20:10). In a general sense, it is all sexual impurity in thought, word, or deed. This is the sense in the Sixth Commandment, interpreted on the principles of the Sermon on the Mount (Exodus 20:14; Deuteronomy 5:18; Matthew 5:27-28). Figuratively, idolatry.

Chapter Seven

Prohibititions And Invitations In The Seventh Commandment

You shall not steal. — Exodus 20:15

If you want to enter life, obey the Commandments [Jesus said].
 "Which ones?" the man [a rich, young man] inquired.
 Jesus replied, "Do not murder, do not commit adultery, do not steal, do not give false testimony, honor your father and mother, and love your neighbor as yourself." — Matthew 19:17-19

A man once sent an unsigned letter to the Internal Revenue Service with no return address. He enclosed a $100 bill. The letter read, "Here is $100 that I owe you. I did not report my income tax return correctly last year. Since then I have not been able to sleep properly. If I still can't sleep, I will send you the rest of the money I owe you."

Oops! Stealing in any form is wrong. We have a Commandment from God about it. It's one of the Big Ten.

Obviously, there is a negative side to the Seventh Commandment. It clearly says, "Don't steal." There is also a positive side that calls for integrity of character like that of Jesus Christ.

Toyohiko Kagawa became a Christian in Japan when he looked at the wonder of Christ, his integrity, his sacrifice, and his love for people. He once described his journey from the world's standards to Christ's standards like this:

> *There once was a man named Jesus*
> *Who went about doing good.*
> *It is very disconcerting to me*
> *That I am so easily occupied with just going about.*

In this chapter we will look at the Bible's negative prohibition against stealing. The Bible teaches that stealing leads to darkness and death. In addition, we will look at the positive invitation in the Bible. Following this invitation leads to life. "If you want to enter life," Jesus says, "obey the Commandments" (Matthew 19:17).

The Negative Prohibition

"You shall not steal." Let's look at four possible implications of this negative prohibition. First, the Seventh Commandment means, "Don't take what doesn't belong to you." Children have to be taught not to take the toys and possessions of others. "It's mine" are words that parents have to confront when children play together. The selfish tendency to grab what doesn't belong to us is evidenced early in life. "But I want it," the child says when a parent says, "You can't have everything you want." Taking what doesn't belong to you is a problem for children. It is also a problem for adults.

A survey shows that at least fifty percent of U.S. employees steal from their employers. Companies report that internal stealing is at epidemic proportions in this country. In many cases, internal security is a bigger problem than security to keep customers from stealing products. Have you heard the excuses that employees caught stealing give?

"It is a big company; they won't miss it."

"They don't pay me enough; this is just my way to get what I deserve."

"The company steals from the public by high prices; why shouldn't I?"

"Everyone does it; why shouldn't I?"

Second, don't get trapped by dishonesty. Chaos is catching; don't succumb. Avoid dishonesty like the plague. Otherwise, it will bring darkness and death to your life. A life-long criminal was asked why he lived a life of crime. He responded, "My parents were dishonest in small things. At first, like them, I was dishonest in small things. Then my dishonesty became an uncontrollable problem. I learned that whenever I got caught, if denial didn't work, one way out was to say 'I'm sorry.' But I wasn't sorry for what I had done. I was really just sorry that I got caught."

Third, "Don't let the world's ethical standards become your standards." Stealing is like a communicable disease. It goes from one person to another and soon becomes a way of life for a high percentage of people all around us. Like Kagawa, mentioned earlier, mold yourself after the standards of Christ, not the standards of those around you. Saint Paul the apostle puts it this way: "Do not conform any longer to the pattern of the world, but be transformed by the renewing of your mind. Then you will be able to test and approve what God's will is — his good, pleasing, and perfect will" (Romans 12:2).

When caught stealing, people often offer lame rationalizations like, "I only did it for a good cause. It may have been wrong, but it was for a good purpose." The "end justifies the means" excuse has been the creed of dishonest minds from the beginning of time. Doctor George Forell was a teacher of ethics at the University of Iowa School of Religion for many years. His insight into the means and ends excuse is significant: "We have control over the means; we do not have control over the ends."

Fourth, "Don't let greed become your creed." Inordinate focus on getting and keeping money is the ruin of many people. The Bible says,

> *People who want to get rich fall into temptation and a trap and into many foolish and harmful desires that plunge men into ruin and destruction. For the love of*

money is a root of all kinds of evil. Some people, eager for money, have wandered from the faith and pierced themselves with many griefs.
— 1 Timothy 6:9-10

The negative emphasis on what not to do is only a partial standard for good living. Let's look at the positive side of this Commandment as well.

The Positive Invitation Of Christ And The Bible

Psalm 112:1 says: "Praise the LORD! Happy are those who fear the LORD, who greatly delight in his Commandments." That is a positive invitation to a meaningful life.

Jesus says, "If you want to enter life, obey the Commandments" (Matthew 19:17). When asked what Commandments he meant, Jesus included obedience to the Commandment about stealing as a way to enjoy life with an eternal dimension. Life with an eternal dimension includes many things. Let's look at four positive aspects of the Seventh Commandment.

First, "Be a man or woman without guile." That means to do what you say and say what you do without game playing. Psychological games include pretending to be better than you are; giving good reasons instead of accurate reasons for what you do; and stealing the reputations of other people by inordinate and inappropriate judgments. A person without guile avoids these psychological games. That person's word is as good as gold. He or she is not a person trying to use people to get what they want, but a person who genuinely tries to help others.

A person without guile seeks the good of others. That kind of person is trustworthy. That kind of person is not preoccupied with self. That kind of person seeks the good of others. Jesus said that Nathaniel was "a man without guile" (John 1:47). We need more people like Nathaniel, in whom there is nothing false.

Martin Luther says that the meaning of this Commandment is that we should have respect and love for God "so that we do not take our neighbor's money or property, or get them in any dishonest way, but help him to improve and protect his property and means of making a living." A person without guile seeks to help his neighbor with his life.

Second, "Show honesty and integrity in all you do." People do not always know what is going on inside us as we speak, but God knows. Honesty and integrity show up at the end of life; so do dishonesty and the lack of integrity. A disciple of Christ seeks to be honest and have integrity in all of life. A Christian with honesty and integrity patterns life after Christ. Jesus said,

> *If anyone would come after me, he must deny himself and take up his cross and follow me. For whoever wants to save his life will lose it, but whoever loses his life for me will find it. What good will it be for a man if he gains the whole world, yet forfeits his soul?*
> — Matthew 16:24-26

Honesty and integrity, or the absence of these qualities, are parts of the mind and soul of every human being. If you have great material gain, but forfeit your soul by shady practices, you will one day have to answer to God for what you have done. Jesus said, "Not everyone who says to me, 'Lord, Lord,' will enter the kingdom of heaven, but he who does the will of my Father who is in heaven" (Matthew 7:21).

What do you do when no one else is looking? That's one way to gauge your honesty and integrity.

Third, "Be just and fair in all your dealings." That means that character is important for Christians. In recent presidential elections, the character, or the lack of it, in the candidates was debated back and forth. The opinion of many in the media was that in the minds of most Americans, character is no longer a major issue when it comes to candidates for high office. If that is true, we are a lost nation. If character doesn't count for those we elect to high office, then we are writing the last chapter in the book, *The Decline And Fall Of America* because without character in our rulers, there will not be justice and fairness in our country.

Fourth, "Give generously to God's work." How is giving generously to God's work a positive expression of the Seventh

Commandment? When you do not give generously, you are stealing from God. Consider the words of Malachi:

> *"Will a man rob God? Yet you rob me." But you ask, "How do we rob you?" "In tithes and offerings. You are under a curse — the whole nation of you — because you are robbing me. Bring the whole tithe into the storehouse, that there may be food in my house. Test me in this," says the LORD Almighty, "and see if I will not throw open the floodgates of heaven and pour out so much blessing that you will not have room enough for it."* — Malachi 3:8-10

Notice the reference to tithes and offerings. One interpretation of this verse is that you don't give offerings until after you have paid the tithe (giving ten percent off the top) to God's work. Giving the tithe is our duty. Giving beyond the tithe is giving generous first-fruit offerings.

As Christians we should certainly not make these words into laws about how much people should give or what percentage of income people should give, but there can be no mistake about it, giving generously does not mean giving leftovers for the work of God. Giving generously is an expression of living life with an eternal dimension. Blessings on blessings from the floodgates of heaven are added to such a life. Such blessings are not always in monetary form. These blessings just mean that we are closer to the heart of God.

In my life there have been many lay people who have served as examples of generous giving. Ada Gleb was one the people in my first church in Lebanon, Indiana, who blessed me with her giving. Ada was poor. She lived in a run-down house. She was retired, living on social security. Nevertheless, she tithed her small income to the work of the Lord. When the mission church needed to put up a church building, Ada doubled her tithe to help make the dream of a worship center a reality. In order to give to the building fund, she had to withdraw money from her small savings account every month.

When Ada died, I learned that she had left me a portion of her savings. The amount was $2,000. Remembering her sacrificial example, there was no way that I could spend the money I received. Instead, the money was given to a bright young woman who would not have been able to attend college without it. That young woman went on to earn a doctorate in biology. Blessings on blessings.

Al Glotfeldty was another person who taught me the meaning of generous giving. Al was a lawyer who gave a lot of his money and time to the work of the church. One day I said to Al, "For every hour you dedicate to the church, you are losing income. As a lawyer you could spend your time on more clients and thus earn more money. Why do you give so much of your money and time to the church?"

Al thought for a moment. Then he replied, "It is all a matter of priorities." Al taught me the importance of putting God's work before making money. In turn, I passed his creed on to others who passed it on to others. Blessings on blessings.

Paul Doddridge is the owner of Connell Chevrolet Company in Costa Mesa, California. He is not only a generous giver to the work of the church, but a man who in his business dealings is known as "a man with integrity." That is really saying a lot for someone whose business is selling cars! If Paul says something, you can take it to the bank. He has blessed many people with his generosity and integrity. Blessings on blessings.

In over forty years of ministry, there have been many people who have been my mentors in the joy of giving generously. Space allows me to mention only these three. These three and many others I have known demonstrate what accepting the invitation of Christ to life with an eternal dimension means.

From the point of view of the gospel, the Seventh Commandment is much more than a negative prohibition against stealing. From the perspective of the cross of Christ, we are called by this Commandment to be persons without guile, with character that can be trusted, producing fruits of honesty and integrity, fairness, and justice. In addition, we are called to be people gripped by the creed of generous giving.

Remembering the words of Kagawa, let us each examine our own lives in the light of Jesus Christ.

There once was a man named Jesus
Who went about doing good.
It is very disconcerting to me
That I am so easily occupied with just going about.

Questions For Your Personal Consideration And/Or Group Discussion

1. My wife once stood at the door of a large department store and with ten single dollar bills in her hand. She dropped them near busy customers who were coming and going. She then asked ten different customers, "Did you drop this dollar?" Most of customers took the money and thanked her for returning the money that they had lost. If you are in a group, discuss what was involved.

2. How can we rob people with our words?

3. What about stealing something small? Read Luke 16:10 before answering.

4. How do we steal other people's ideas?

5. Have you ever been robbed? How does it feel?

6. Do you agree or disagree with this statement: "Other people should never be exploited to further my gain"?

Digging Deeper

1. When caught stealing, people often play the game, "P.T.B." (Pass The Buck). Read about passing the buck in Genesis 3:12-13.

2. Consider the many aspects of the Seventh Commandment, including cheating on income taxes, cheating in school, and the distorted desire for material things.

3. In the light of the Seventh Commandment, consider Communism, *laissez-faire* capitalism, and other aspects of economic life.

4. Kagawa, as a result of his faith in Christ, went to the slums of Kobe, Japan, to live as a Christ figure among the poor. On December 24, 1909, Kagawa moved into a shack in the inner city. On December 25, a knock at the door brought Kagawa face to face with a man with a dreaded skin disease who asked, "What are you doing here?" Kagawa replied, "I live here." The man looked around and said, "Do you live alone?" Getting a positive reply, he stepped into the tiny room and said, "This is much too big a place for one person. I'll come and live with you." Thus began the story of one of the most Christlike men in the twentieth century.

5. Consider the prohibitions of the Seventh Commandment:
    a. Don't take what doesn't belong to you.
    b. Don't get trapped by dishonesty.
    c. Don't let the world's standard of cheating become your standard.
    d. Don't let greed become your creed.

6. Consider the invitation of the Bible and Christ regarding the Seventh Commandment:
   a. Be a man or woman without guile.
   b. Show honesty and integrity in all you do.
   c. Be just and fair in your dealings.
   d. Give generously to God's work.

7. Discuss the story Pastor Dianne Eller once told about a Native American man who said, "There are two dogs in my heart. The one is a bad dog. The other is a good dog. They are always fighting." When asked which dog won the battles, he replied, "The one I feed."

Chapter Eight

Prohibition And Invitations In The Eighth Commandment

You shall not give false testimony against your neighbor.   — Exodus 20:16

Do not judge, or you too will be judged. For in the same way you judge others, you will be judged, and with the measure you use, it will be measured to you. Why do you look at the speck of sawdust in your brother's eye and pay no attention to the plank in your own eye? How can you say to your brother, "Let me take the speck out of your eye," when all the time there is a plank in your own eye? You hypocrite, first take the plank out of your own eye, and then you will see clearly to remove the speck from your brother's eye.
— Matthew 7:1-5

Martin Luther says that the meaning of the Eighth Commandment is:

> *We are to fear and love God so that we do not betray, slander, or lie about our neighbor, but defend him, speak well of him, and explain his actions in the kindest way.*[13]

In his interpretation, Luther gives us two sides of the meaning of the Eighth Commandment: 1) a prohibition against betraying, slandering, and lying and 2) the invitation to a high quality of life by putting a charitable interpretation on our neighbor's behavior.

The Prohibition Against Lying, Betraying, And Slandering

Why do people lie? Some people do it to get revenge. They have been hurt by someone. They return a hurt for a hurt by telling some untruth about the person who hurt them. However, returning hurt for hurt often results in the object of their lies returning lies for lies.

Some people lie to make themselves look better. By stretching the truth about someone, they think they are elevating themselves. However, while pointing at someone else with one finger, they are pointing three others back at themselves.

Some people lie because they believe the object of their lies deserves punishment. Perhaps the object of the lies is in an important position. The liar thinks, "Maybe this will bring them down a peg or two." However, the lie brings the liar down more than a peg or two.

Some people are liars because after telling so many lies, they can no longer distinguish the truth from a lie. Like a snowball going downhill, lying gets so large that it is soon unmanageable.

Some people lie to rationalize their own behavior, to save themselves from some consequence they want to avoid. To rationalize means to give a good reason instead of the real reason for what we have done. Not honestly facing something that they have done or said results in not repenting. Not repenting compounds trouble between the liar and God, and between the liar and other people.

Lying includes duplicity, false judgments, exaggerations, falsifications, fabrications, concoctions, misrepresentations, and rationalizations. One of the main troubles with lying is that it always leads to more lies to cover the original ones. When you tell the truth, it is not hard to remember what you said. When you lie, it is easy to forget what you said. Then you have to cover one lie with others. What tangled webs we weave when we try to deceive.

In a court of law we are told to avoid perjury. The question asked of those who mount the witness stand while putting a hand on the Bible is: "Do you swear to tell the truth, the whole truth, and nothing but the truth, so help you God?" The Eighth Commandment lays a foundation for law by telling us not to give false testimony against our neighbors.

Jesus extends the meaning of the Eighth Commandment by including false and quick judgment of other people who have only a speck in their eyes, while not noticing that we have a two by twelve plank coming out of our own eyes. To put down others while ignoring our own faults is a way to break this Commandment. When you stop to think of it that way, none of us is free from breaking the Eighth Commandment.

If you still have trouble seeing how this Commandment relates to your life, consider the values of the society in which we live. Today, many people have lowered moral expectations related to this Commandment. They expect people to lie if it suits their purposes. Society has become complacent about lying. Consider this complacency as it relates to distorted individuality, corrupted free speech, ruthless free enterprise, and ethical relativism.

Individuality can be a good thing. Inordinate individuality isn't good. Inordinate individuality means that my position is right; your position wrong. In order to preserve my opinion, a voice in my head suggests that lying may be justified.

Free speech is a good thing. A distorted emphasis on free speech can result in people thinking that they can say whatever comes to their minds, no matter how it hurts others.

Free enterprise is a good thing, but winning at all costs may mean that people think that it is okay to distort the truth in any way that is necessary to keep them on an upwardly mobile pattern. Individual rights are protected by our constitution, but claiming rights without exercising responsibility results in chaos.

Ethical relativism has resulted in eliminating all absolute standards, including the absolute standard of God's Commandments. However, when you eliminate the Eighth Commandment as a standard that all people should follow, you can no longer depend on what people tell you. If personal choice is elevated to the highest level in a distorted way, then telling the truth or telling lies becomes little more than a choice between whether you like pizza and beer, or Swedish meatballs and ludefisk. When it comes to lying or telling the truth, we have an absolute truth from God about what is best. Bearing false witness is included in God's Big Ten, not to inhibit freedom but to join freedom with responsibility.

Who would be so foolish as to challenge the importance of freedom? Yet the use of my freedom to do as I please can result in serious damage to others. Luther described the paradox of freedom and responsibility like this: "The Christian is a perfectly free man, subject to no one and a perfectly bound man subject to everyone." Abuse of personal freedom results in bondage of others. That is not what our founding fathers had in mind when they advocated liberty.

We have a Statue of Liberty on the east coast. Why not add a Statue of Responsibility on the west coast? That way we would show that we live in the tension between liberty and responsibility.

Liars diminish themselves as they try to diminish others. The book of James describes the damage that results from lying and bearing false witness against the neighbor. The image of a ship's rudder and a forest fire are used to drive home the need to tame the tongue.

> *... Take ships as an example. Although they are so large and are driven by strong winds, they are steered by a very small rudder wherever the pilot wants to go.*
> — James 3:4

> *... The tongue is a small part of the body, but it makes great boasts. Consider what a great forest is set on fire by a small spark. The tongue also is a fire, a world of evil among the parts of the body. It corrupts the whole person, sets the whole course of his life on fire, and is itself set on fire by hell.* — James 3:5-6

Adolf Hitler said that if you tell a big lie often enough, many people will believe it. He told a big lie about the Jews. Many Jews were killed because of the lies and propaganda of the Nazis.

Hate gains longevity through lies. "Evil-speak" in all forms is dangerous.

The Eighth Commandment is a serious negative prohibition. It is also a positive invitation to a high-quality life. We are called to be kind in our interpretations of what our neighbors say and do.

The Invitation To Put A Charitable Interpretation On The Actions Of Others

All forms of "evil-speak" are wrong in the sight of God. On the other hand, the Lord rejoices when we follow the example of Jesus Christ in our treatment of other people. We are called to put the most charitable interpretation on our neighbor's behavior.

In the time of Jesus, the Jews hated the Samaritans, a half-breed race that was formed when most of the Jews were deported to Babylon in 586 B.C. Many Samaritans were caught in the trap of idolatry, yet Jesus told a story with a good Samaritan as the hero because he stopped to help his neighbor. Jesus did not approve of the behavior of the Samaritans who had forgotten their monotheistic heritage. He just drew a big enough circle to include any of them who would come to him as Lord and Savior.

According to John 4:1-42, Jesus put a positive interpretation on the faith of the Samaritan woman at the well, not because he approved of her behavior of living with a man who was not her husband, but because he saw that light of potential faith in her eyes that others did not see. He gave her a chance at a new life. As a result, she brought many other Samaritans to listen to him and they in turn were converted. In order to win these souls, Jesus had to see the Samaritans as potential believers. Jesus accepted people without accepting their bad behavior.

When Jesus talked about judging others for having a small piece of sawdust in their eyes while not seeing the plank coming out of our own eyes, he was doing more than condemning hypocrites. He was offering a vision of a high-quality life where people could see the potential in other people through the eyes of God.

When Jesus told us to love our enemies, he was inviting us to turn enemies into friends by the way we speak of them and about them. He was inviting us to avoid unnecessary put-downs, but he was also inviting us to learn to speak the truth in love.

Think of it this way: God has a picture of each of his children in his wallet. Like a proud father, he gladly shows each picture to anyone who will look at it. Then pointing to one at a time he says, "That's one of mine." Whenever we gossip or bear false witness against his children, we are hurting the heavenly Father who loves them. Jesus said, "As you have done it to the least of these my children, you have done it to me."

For my sins of speech and deeds there is no excuse. When I see my sins, I should not excuse myself for them. My only option is to repent and ask God's help so as not to repeat the evil I have committed. For your sins, I should be more charitable. Instead of pretending to be your God and judge, I am called to speak well of you and put as positive an interpretation on what you say and do as I can. I am called to explain your actions in a kind way.

Instead, the human tendency is to find excuses for my behavior and be critical of yours. That is why the answer to the question, "Does this Commandment relate to me?" is, "It certainly does." The positive application of the Eighth Commandment is to put a charitable interpretation on your actions.

When others are putting you down, I am called to speak up for you and talk about the good parts of you that others ignore. Of course, that doesn't mean that I ignore the evil I see around me, just that I am called to try to find possible explanations for the behavior of others. I dare not apply excuses to myself, lest I get caught in the trap of self-deception and rationalization.

In other words, I am called to try to see everyone through God's eyes. More particularly, I am called to see you through God's eyes.

Questions For Personal Consideration And/Or Group Discussion

1. If you are in a group, discuss lying in advertising and politics.

2. Is it okay to lie on a resume because you really need a job?

3. What problems are involved in lying to a spouse or children?

4. Read 1 Samuel 20:28 and Exodus 1:15-22. Discuss this statement: "Lying is never right, but sometimes as in the case of saving someone else's life, it may be the best of several bad options."

5. When is withholding information lying?

6. When is withholding information not lying?

7. How can false flattery hurt other people?

8. What is wrong with this excuse for lying? "The ends justify the means."

Digging Deeper

1. "Honesty means that everything you say must be true, not that everything you think must be said" (Anonymous).

2. Think before you speak. You may feel that something is true only to find out later that it is false. A quick tongue can get you into trouble.

3. A mature Christian monitored speech and behavior like this: "If I know something I am about to say or do is for the benefit of others and glorifies God, I try to say or do it. If I know that what I am about to say or do is contrary to God and his Word, I try not to say or do it. If I am not sure, I try to wait."

4. We can't be sure that a "little lie" (a "white lie") will be harmless. We can't be sure about the results of lies of any size or color.

5. It is not necessary to reveal your every opinion, perception, reaction, preference, or fantasy. Some things are better kept to ourselves.

6. Consider Psalm 10:3-11 and Psalm 14:2-3.

7. The truth about lying is that it feeds dysfunction and leads to death. Duplicity is what Devlin Donaldson, co-author of *Pinocchio Nation*, calls "a little death." Donaldson adds, "We've got to break that (lying) habit. We've got to tell the truth about the little things and then other times, we'll have the strength, the character, the will, to tell the truth about the consequential things."

8. Bill Clinton, former president of the most powerful nation in the world, acted in a childish manner when he lied on national television about himself and Monica Lewinsky. Leaders of nations, businesses, institutions of learning, churches, and families, isn't it time to stop lying? Isn't it time to stand up and tell the truth? Isn't it time to quit bearing false witness and start putting a charitable interpretation on our neighbors' behavior? After all, the children and youth are watching. More importantly, God is watching.

9. Consider the meaning of this anonymous poem.

> **Don't Judge Others Too Hard**
> *Pray do not find fault with the man who limps,*
> *Or stumbles along the way,*
> *Unless you have worn the shoes that he wears,*
> *Or struggled beneath his sway.*
>
> *There may be tacks in his shoes that hurt*
> *Though hidden away from view,*
> *Or the burden he bears, placed on your back*
> *Might cause you to stumble, too.*
>
> *Don't sneer at the man who's down today,*
> *Unless you have felt the blow*
> *That caused his fall, or felt the shame*
> *That only the fallen know.*
>
> *You may be strong, but still the blows*
> *That were his, if dealt to you*
> *In the self-same way at the self-same time,*
> *Might cause you to stagger, too.*
>
> *Don't be harsh with the man who sins*
> *Or pelt him with word or stone*
> *Unless you are sure, yea doubly sure*
> *That you have no sins of your own.*

*For, perhaps, if the tempter's voice
Should whisper as soft to you
As it did to him when he went astray,
You would falter, too!*

— Author Unknown

Chapter Nine

Prohibitions And Invitations In The Ninth Commandment

You shall not covet your neighbor's house.
— Exodus 20:17a

Do not store up for yourselves treasures on earth, where moth and rust destroy, and where thieves break in and steal. But store up for yourselves treasures in heaven, where moth and rust do not destroy, and where thieves do no break in and steal. For where your treasure is, there your heart will be also. — Matthew 6:19-21

Do not let your hearts be troubled. Trust in God; trust also in me. In my Father's house are many rooms; if it were not so, I would have told you. I am going there to prepare a place for you. — John 14:1-2

Thomas Aquinas once observed: "We were created so that we would love people and use things. The nature of sin is that we love things and use people." Aquinas was describing the malady of coveting. To love things more than people is to totally reverse God's intentions for us.

Coveting is inordinate wanting or wishing for something, especially something that belongs to another. This inordinate wanting keeps you from being happy with what you have. It is wanting at someone else's expense, wanting what someone else has, or more than someone else has. Unrestrained, this inordinate wanting can become an obsession and easily take over a person's life. In God's Big Ten the prohibition against coveting is clear.

Jesus retains this prohibition. He says, "Do not think that I have come to abolish the Law or the Prophets; I have not come to abolish them but to fulfill them" (Matthew 5:17). In addition, Jesus adds invitations to a better life by focusing on God and people instead of things. In this chapter we will look at both prohibitions and invitations in this Commandment, especially as they relate to our neighbor's house.

Prohibitions

How shall we consider the prohibitions that come with the Ninth Commandment? Lets look at seven possible prohibitions related to coveting in general and prohibitions about our neighbor's house in particular.

First, this Commandment deals with desires gone astray. Desires are not evil of themselves. On the contrary, God expects us to be passionate about life, not dull or stale. The question is what things are we called to be passionate about and what things become dangerous as we get all heated up about them? Simply put, we are called to be passionate about God and his kingdom, and to be passionate with love for people, even our enemies. Because we are by nature sinful, it is easy to fall into the trap of trying to outdo our neighbor in the area of housing.

It is not wrong to want a nice house, but desire for a bigger and better house than our neighbor's always gets us into trouble. Excessive desire for expensive furnishings or an unhealthy desire for better lawns and gardens than others have is the kind of coveting included in this Commandment. Desires like these start small, but grow as we make comparisons. They can become uncontrollable as we "try to keep up with the Joneses." Prohibition number one is about desires gone astray.

Second, this Commandment deals with motivations. Why do we want a house in a certain neighborhood or price bracket? Sometimes the motivation is to have a good school for our children.

Sometimes we are just trying to make a good investment that will benefit our family in the long run. But sometimes the motivation is not pure. Why do people often get in over their heads financially when it comes to buying and furnishing a home? People are often motivated by secret thoughts and feelings of wanting to be better than others. These feelings are secrets which can make us sick. The second prohibition is to be careful not to fall into the trap of motivations that make us sick.

Third, the Eighth Commandment deals with the prohibition against envy. According to Proverbs 14:30, envy is like a cancer in the bones. It consumes us. Envy for the kind of possessions others have is dangerous. Jesus said, "Take heed, and beware of all covetousness, for a man's life does not consist in the abundance of his possessions" (Luke 12:15 RSV). Desire for bigger and better houses is often a matter of envy. Envy causes us trouble.

Fourth, covetousness is a prohibition about jealousy. Jealousy regarding houses and furnishings that family, friends, or neighbors have can cause big trouble in relationships. One of the big reasons for divorce today is money problems caused by trying to catch up to or get ahead of someone else. Jealousy is a fact of life used by unscrupulous promoters to get buyers to go beyond what they can manage.

Fifth, covetousness is prohibited because it is based on selfishness. In a recent game of Monopoly with my grandsons, these fine young men moved from healthy competition to ruthless capitalism in buying toy houses and hotels in order to put the other players out of business. One minute the boys were laughing and teasing one another about the game; the next they were fighting and shouting to gain advantage over their opponents. We stopped the game and talked about what had happened. Our grandsons could see that the game had turned into a miniature version of what happens when wealthy and selfish business people grind out their success at the expense of other people. Selfishness means excessive concentration on holding or gaining one's own advantage at the expense of others. The biblical prohibitions about selfishness are clear. "Do nothing out of selfish ambition or vain conceit," Paul writes (Philippians 2:3).

Sixth, covetousness means greed. Greed has become such a creed in our time that we hardly see it as a problem. The stranglehold of materialism is such that media news of a bad economy often implies that there is something wrong with consumers who are not buying homes and household goods (and other things) at the rate they did the previous year. The implication? Consumers should feel guilty about not buying major and minor items to keep the economy hot. The Bible prohibits greed as a creed for life.

Seventh, the Ninth Commandment prohibition against covetousness deals with the difference between want and need. Luxuries for the home have become necessities in the minds of many today. Excessive credit buying has become an obsession with many. High interest payments on remaining balances drives an insurmountable wedge into many family budgets.

The Ninth Commandment gives us warnings about all of these aspects of covetousness. But there are more than prohibitions here. The Bible also offers us invitations to see true values from a higher perspective.

Invitations

From the high perspective of the kingdom of God, we can see things as they really are, not as they seem to be. Consider four biblical invitations that relate to the Ninth Commandment.

The first biblical invitation is to consider the location of our real home. The words of Jesus about storing up treasures that last are an invitation to see the home where we will spend eternity. He says, "... store up for yourselves treasures in heaven ... for where your treasure is, there your heart will be also" (Matthew 6:20-21). That is a positive invitation to see heaven as our real home.

The book of Hebrews puts it this way: "... here we do not have an enduring city, but we are looking for the city that is to come" (Hebrews 13:14). Let me paraphrase that verse in the context of the Ninth Commandment. "In the journey through life, we are invited to see and embrace the lasting home God has provided for us in eternity."

The second invitation implied by this Commandment is an invitation to contentment. Jesus says, "Do not let your hearts be troubled. Trust in God; trust also in me. In my Father's house are many rooms; if it were not so, I would have told you. I am going to prepare a place for you" (John 14:1-2). Let me paraphrase that in the light of the theme of this chapter. "You can have contentment and peace in your hearts instead of being all steamed up about getting something bigger and better than your neighbors."

The Alcoholics Anonymous Serenity Prayer can help us make decisions about when to act and when to relax, be content and serene, and simply trust God.

God, grant me the serenity to accept the things I cannot change;
courage to change the things I can;
and wisdom to know the difference.

The third biblical invitation related to this Commandment is the invitation to set the priorities that will bring this kind of contentment. Jesus put it this way, "Seek first the kingdom of God ..." (Matthew 6:25).

The story of Zacchaeus (Luke 19:1-9) is the story of a man who initially had priorities all mixed up. He was a tax collector who robbed and cheated to line his own pockets. He got the things of this world, but was out of touch with his heavenly home and personal contentment until Jesus came along and stayed at his house. The light dawned on him when Jesus came for a visit. Zacchaeus saw the error of trying to have bigger and better houses and possessions. On the spot he reordered his priorities. "Look, Lord," he said, "Here and now I give half of my possessions to the poor, and if I have cheated anybody out of anything, I will pay back four times the amount" (Luke 19:8). He accepted Jesus' invitation to see things the way God sees them.

The fourth biblical invitation is to know the secret of both having and not having the things of this world. I like the way that Saint Paul describes that secret. "... I have learned, in whatever state I am, to be content. I know how to be abased (be down), and I know how to abound (be up); in any and all circumstances I have learned the secret of facing plenty and hunger, abundance and want"

(Philippians 4:11-12 RSV). Then he goes on to reveal that secret: "I can do all things in him (Christ) who strengthens me" (Philippians 4:13 RSV).

The Ninth Commandment warns us about the dangers of coveting our neighbor's house, but the Bible gives us more than warnings in this area. The Bible gives us invitations to life:

- Know that your real home is heaven.
- Be content with what you have.
- Set priorities with God's kingdom being the highest of all priorities.
- Know and practice the biblical secret of contentment which is to do all that you do in Christ.

Questions For Your Personal Consideration And/Or Group Discussion

1. "When you get what you want, you no longer want what you have gotten. You want more."
   Do you agree or disagree with this statement?

2. There is a fine line between wanting a nice house, furnishings, lawn, garden, and the like, and coveting something someone else has.
   What are some of the ingredients that go into inordinate and excessive wanting?

3. Proverbs 14:30 says: "A heart at peace gives life to the body, but envy rots the bones."
   In what ways can envy be hurtful physically as well as mentally and spiritually?

4. How do people live out, "Greed is my creed"?

5. What are some of the differences between want and need?

Digging Deeper

1. To have a permanent home in heaven means that we do not put our roots down here on earth. It means to recognize that life comes to an end for all of us. It means that all of us must face God and face up to what we have believed and done. It means that there is a vertical as well as a horizontal dimension to life. While it is possible to be so heavenly minded that we are no earthly good, it is also possible to be so earthly minded that we have no heavenly focus, acting as if we will live on earth forever.

2. To be at peace and have contentment about our dwelling place on earth does not mean that we never move to better homes, only that we are not driven to get bigger and better places than others have.

3. The three most significant leaders in the Bible — Jesus, Moses, and Abraham — did not have permanent residences here on earth. They were people on the move who saw that their permanent home was with God.

4. According to the Bible, these should be our priorities in life:
   a. God and his kingdom;
   b. spouse;
   c. children and family; and
   d. profession or job resulting in income.

Chapter Ten

Prohibitions And Invitations In The Tenth Commandment

You shall not covet your neighbor's wife, or his manservant or maidservant, his ox or donkey, or anything that belongs to your neighbor. — Exodus 20:17b

Take heed; and beware of all covetousness; for a man's life does not consist in the abundance of his possessions. — Luke 12:15 (RSV)

... I have learned, in whatever state I am, to be content. I know how to be abased and I know how to abound; in any and all circumstances I have learned the secret of facing plenty and hunger, abundance and want. I can do all things in him [Christ] who strengthens me." — Philippians 4:11-13 (RSV)

Some time ago I was preaching a sermon on covetousness, referencing the Tenth Commandment. Trying to be honest about the items listed in the Tenth Commandment (Exodus 20:17b: wives, menservants, maidservants, and cattle), but at the same time add a little levity to the sermon, I asked the question, "How many of you lusted after cattle on your way to church today?"

About halfway down the aisle on the right side of the church, Charlie, a bold parishioner, raised his hand and shouted out an answer to my question. "I did it. I'm guilty. I looked at a herd of my neighbor's cattle on the way to church and coveted what he had." Charlie was the manager of the University of Arizona Dairy Farm in Tucson, Arizona. He is now my son-in-law. Thanks for the honesty, Charlie.

The original cultural context and the particulars of this Commandment may be different than the cultural context and particulars today, but the meaning is the same. Therefore, we will focus here on "... anything that belongs to your neighbor" (Exodus 20:17b) and "... beware of all covetousness ..." (Luke 12:15 RSV).

Let's Review

As noted earlier in this book, the Bible does not number the Ten Commandments. Jews and Protestants number the Ten Commandments in one way with two Commandments on idolatry; Lutherans and Roman Catholics number them in a different way with two Commandments on covetousness. Since I am a Lutheran, I stick with the latter numbering.

As noted in the last chapter, coveting is inordinate wanting or wishing for something, especially something that belongs to another. As noted, there are at least seven prohibitions against coveting in the Bible.

1. Avoid desires gone astray.
2. Check your motivations regarding covetousness.
3. Watch out for envy. Envy can consume you.
4. Don't let jealousy rule. Jealousy is a fact of life, but it is dangerous.
5. Check the level of your selfishness. Covetousness is based on selfishness.
6. Re-evaluate your creed. Greed as a creed has become a way of life for many modern Americans.
7. Show wisdom as you examine the difference between wants and needs. Some things that you feel you must have, are only wants without which you can get along fine.

All of these prohibitions apply to the Tenth Commandment as well as the Ninth. In addition, the four invitations discussed in the last chapter apply to the Tenth Commandment as well as the Ninth. The Bible invites us to:

1. Know that our real home is with God.
2. Be content with what we have instead of lusting after what someone else has.
3. Set priorities with God's kingdom in first place.
4. Remember and practice the biblical secret of doing all things in Christ who strengthens us.

In this chapter we will focus on the meaning of the biblical secret of doing all things in Christ who strengthens us.

How To Be Abased

Saint Paul learned the secret of being abased. To be abased means to be lower physically or in the minds of others as to office, place, rank, prestige, or esteem. That happened to Paul. As he wrote the letter to his Philippian friends, Paul was in prison (house arrest) in Rome for preaching the gospel of salvation through Jesus Christ. Being considered a criminal would usually make a person feel dejected and defeated. Not Paul. He knew the secret of handling things that cause most people to feel depressed. He knew how to be abased.

Paul had a big problem which he called "his thorn in the flesh" (2 Corinthians 12:7). Some scholars think that it was epilepsy; others think that Paul had a problem with painful headaches and eye trouble. Some have theorized that Paul's thorn was carnal temptation. No one knows, but what we do know is that pain accompanied Paul wherever he went and threatened to limit his ministry. Others with similar problems succumb. Not Paul. He overcame his problem. He learned how to be abased.

Paul sensed that he was near the end of his road, near death. As people near this point in life, they often feel "lower than a snake's belly," as one dying patient told me. Not Paul. He not only knew the secret of overcoming death. He knew how to be abased. At the end of his life, what did Paul have by way of the world's material goods? Not much. As a matter of fact, he had next to nothing. Not only did he have next to nothing by worldly standards; even most of his Christian friends seemed to have abandoned him. Only Timothy seems to be there when Paul needs him. "I have no one else like him (Timothy) who takes a genuine interest in your welfare," Paul wrote. "For everyone looks out for his own interests, not those of Jesus Christ" (Philippians 2:20-21). Ever feel that you have been short-changed in the marketplace of money and things? Ever feel that you have been forgotten by family or friends or fellow workers? Paul felt that way, too, but he overcame resentments that defeat many people by turning to the secret of handling negative feelings. He knew how to be abased.

What is the secret of handling the really tough aspects of life? What is the secret of overcoming those times that cause the majority of people to give up? Paul puts it simply: "I have learned the secret of being abased ... I can do all things in Christ who strengthens me."

The secret of the Christian life is giving attention to God and his ways. What gets your attention, gets you. If you give your attention to the acquisition of material goods, material goods will get you. That, in the last analysis, is what coveting is all about — giving inordinate attention to the wrong things.

Some demonic scoundrel has crawled into the show window of life and moved the price tags. The cheap things have been given high price tags; the valuable things low price tags. When you believe the devil's tricks and illusions, materialism becomes a way of life. When you see the devil's tricks and illusions for what they are, you get a proper perspective on the things of this world. The secret of being abased is giving your attention to God. What gets your attention, gets you. When everything around him was coming unglued, Paul turned his attention to good and godly things.

The secret of the Christian life is focus. Paul describes the focus that overcomes trouble like this: "... whatever is noble, whatever is right, whatever is pure, whatever is lovely, whatever is admirable — if anything is excellent or praiseworthy — think about such things" (Philippians 4:8-9). Paul's thinking was about Christ and his teachings. His thinking was about the high and the holy so he did not succumb to the temptations of the low and ungodly things of life.

"I know what it is to be in need," Paul wrote (Philippians 4:12). I didn't just read about it in a book or learn about it from others' experience. I have been there. That is where I am right now. But it makes no difference. My mind is on the high things of God and no one can take that from me. No one.

Paul knew the secret of being abased. He gave his attention and focus to Christ. He also knew how to abound.

How To Abound

"No one needs to teach me how to be rich and have things in abundance," a rich and stubborn business man once told me. "I know how to do that." Wrong. Most people can't handle success. Most are miserable when they get what they think they want. Most fumble the ball as they cross the goal line of prosperity. Covetousness sets in like a cancer. Covetous people no longer want what they have gotten. They want more.

Paul knew the secret of success. He knew how to handle prosperity. He knew how to abound. "I know what it is to have plenty," he writes (Philippians 4:12). To be copiously supplied with the world's goods generally works havoc on people. Many lose their way when the quantity of things goes way up. Many cannot handle abounding. Many forget to be grateful to God for what they have. They think, "My strong arm or mighty mind has gotten me this victory." Wrong.

The secret of success is gratitude to God. Without gratitude, every worldly success turns to dust. Without gratitude, prosperity turns to sickness. Without gratitude, treasures become burdens. Without gratitude, an attitude of griping enters the soul.

In my book *Turning Griping Into Gratitude*,[14] the secret of the psalmists is revealed. They learned to focus on God in time of trouble and prosperity.

Gratitude is the heart of Christian stewardship. Stewardship is not primarily a matter of duty. It is not primarily a matter of giving money to a church budget. Christian stewardship is what we do with our lives after we say "Yes," to Jesus Christ. When Christ comes into our lives, we should become grateful givers.

John was a church member, but he wasn't really grateful for what God had done for him until he had a heart attack. That woke him up. Emily, John's wife, was grateful for John's change of heart, but she had a problem. She won $3 million in the state lottery, and was afraid to tell John for fear that he would get excited, have another heart attack, and die. She asked for assistance from her pastor.

The pastor said to John, "In your mind, I want you to picture $3 million far away. John, do you see it?"

"Yes," John said. "I see it."

"Now, John, picture the $3 million coming closer. Do you see it?"

"No problem, Pastor. I see it."

"Now, John, what would you do with $3 million if you actually received it?"

John thought for a moment and then replied, "I'd give half of it to the church."

On hearing this, the pastor dropped dead with a heart attack.

Pastors rarely experience such generosity. Genuine gratitude to God expressed through giving to the church and the needs of other people is rare. It surprises us when it comes.

Most people cannot handle prosperity. It goes to their heads. In our day, coveting often includes a distorted evaluation of things like cars, boats, and recreational vehicles. On the back bumper of an expensive RV, this message appeared: "In the end, the one with the most toys wins." Wrong. In the end, the only thing that counts is whether or not we have a relationship with God through Jesus Christ.

Most people turn in on themselves when riches come. A wealthy member of one of the churches I served was severely depressed in spite of the fact that she had everything most people want. Her husband made a good income as an executive with a large company. They lived in a beautiful new home. She had jewelry and clothes far beyond what others had. They drove big, expensive cars. Nevertheless, she was depressed and went to a psychiatrist for help. She told me, "The psychiatrist is not really helping me. Why don't you phone him and see if you can find out what you can?" I agreed to phone the psychiatrist. He said, "Nobody can help her. She is a faded, jaded narcissist." Wow! That's a condition that only God can correct.

There is a poem that describes the problem and the solution.

Said the Robin to the Sparrow,
"I should really like to know
Why these human beings rush about
And worry so."

Said the Sparrow to the Robin,
"Friend, I think that it must be
That they have no Heavenly Father
Such as cares for you and me."
— Elizabeth Cheney

In this chapter we have focused on the prohibitions and invitations of God regarding covetousness. Ask yourself, "How does all of this make a difference to me?" Then think about what materialism really means.

You plus money equals nothing in the end. You plus power equals nothing when you die. But you plus God — that's an unconquerable partnership for this life and the next.

Questions For Your Personal Consideration
And/Or Group Discussion

1. Read Matthew 6:25-33. What do lilies have to do with real life?

2. Consider Soren Kierkegaard's story of a lily and a bird.
    A lily, growing in all it's natural beauty was quite content until a bird happened by and indicated that perhaps the open field just wasn't the best place for the flower to develop to it's full potential. The bird told the lily about a beautiful garden and the wonderful lilies that grew there. Since the little flower wanted to be the most beautiful lily in the world, a plan was conceived. One day the bird came and dug around the roots of the lily to free it. When the little lily was free, the bird took it in it's bill and began to fly to the beautiful garden. By the time it got there, the lily was dead.

3. Consider the story of a caterpillar named Stripe.
    Stripe crawled along the ground; yet he felt an urge to get up high. Stripe was aggressive, so he was uncomfortable with this unfulfilled urge. One day Stripe found something to climb. It was a caterpillar pillar. Other caterpillars were climbing this caterpillar pillar. Stripe decided to climb it, too. About half way up the climbing got rough. Stripe stepped on the head of another caterpillar.
    "I'm sorry," he said. "What's your name?"
    "My name is 'Yellow,' " she replied.
    "I'm sorry, Yellow, I hope I didn't hurt you."
    On up, up, up Stripe went. Then he heard a voice . The voice said, "The only way to get higher is to push others aside."
    After a while, Stripe got tired of all the pushing, so he started down. When he saw Yellow, he invited her to come along on the descent. She agreed. They found a nice home in

the soft grass and lived quite happily, but only for a short time. Stripe still felt the strong urge to go up.

One day when Yellow was basking in the sun, Stripe told her that he was going back to the pillar of caterpillars. Up, up, up, he went, this time more determined than ever to get to the top, no matter what the cost. As he pushed and shoved and stepped on other caterpillars, Stripe got closer to the top. Then he heard something strange. One of the caterpillars near the top said, "There's nothing here."

Stripe thought that the caterpillar who spoke was just trying to keep the others from getting to the top so he disregarded the remark. Again he heard the voice, "There's nothing here, nothing at all." Again, he disregarded the remark.

Then he heard another voice. "The only way to get to the top is to push those on the top off." Like the others near the top, Stripe pushed and pushed. He saw several other caterpillars falling. "Good," he thought. "Make room for me."

He looked down. He saw the mass of caterpillars on the pillar and on the ground. He looked out and saw caterpillar pillars everywhere. "What does this mean?" he asked.

Just then Stripe saw a butterfly — a little yellow butterfly that seemed to be beckoning him down. Slowly he descended the pillar. The yellow butterfly led him over to the soft grass where he had enjoyed life with Yellow. Then she led him to a tree and a special branch with a cocoon on it. Suddenly, Stripe knew the meaning of the urge to go up. (Adapted from *Hope For The Flowers* by Trina Paulus.)

Digging Deeper

1. Covetousness is a poison that enters the blood stream and then slowly kills us.

2. Read 1 Corinthians 7:31. If this verse is true and the world as we know it is passing away, why would anyone devote himself/herself to it?

3. "Not everyone who says to me, 'Lord, Lord,' will enter the kingdom of heaven, but only he who does the will of my Father who is in heaven" (Matthew 7:21).

4. A pastor sat next to beautiful young woman on a 747 flight from one end of the country to the other. He asked her what she did for a living. "I'm a flight attendant," she said. "I'm just traveling across the country so that I can work on a plane out of Los Angeles."
    Then the pastor inquired further about her life. "It will be a long flight across the country. Why don't you tell me about yourself?"
    "Oh," she replied, "I live with my boyfriend in Los Angeles. We've been together three years now. What do you do for a living?"
    "I'm a minister."
    "Oh," she gulped. "I suppose you think it's sinful for me to live with a man who isn't my husband."
    "I don't exactly recommend it."
    Then something changed in the conversation. The flight attendant began reflecting on the fact that she had had a little religious training as a child, but had drifted away from it. Suddenly she turned to the minister and said, "Tell me about life after death. My boyfriend says that eternal life is just something people made up because they are afraid of dying. He says that this life is all there is."

    For several hours the pastor told her about Jesus Christ and his gift of eternal life for those who believe. They talked about faith in God and what it really means.

    "Thanks," the flight attendant said as she got off the plane. "You have really helped me with answers to many of my questions. I'm not sure how my boyfriend will react, but I am going to try faith in God and start going to church whenever I can."

    The minister concluded about the experience: "Even people who have no apparent interest in religion are longing for some word of hope about the difference between the 'rat race' in this life and eternal life. That Jesus Christ gives us the last word, his word, about these matters has something to say to everyone, even apparently disinterested secularists."

5. H. George Anderson, former Presiding Bishop of the Evangelical Lutheran Church in America, says that greed is often disguised as "a plea for fairness." An example he sites is when people are determined to get their "fair share" of an inheritance. This determination can become compulsive.

    "Another disguise greed takes," he says, "is ambition." The normal drive to succeed can become blind ambition.

6. Jesus said, "Take care! Be on your guard against all kinds of greed; for one's life does not consist in the abundance of possessions" (Luke 12:15 NRSV).

The Eleventh Commandment

Chapter Eleven

Prohibitions And Invitations In The Eleventh Commandment

One of the teachers of the law came and heard them debating. Noticing that Jesus had given them (the Sadducees) a good answer, he asked him, "Of all the Commandments, which is the most important?"

"The most important one," answered Jesus, "is this: 'Hear, O Israel, the Lord our God, the Lord is one. Love the Lord your God with all your heart and with all your soul and with all your mind and with all your strength.' The second is this: 'Love your neighbor as yourself.' There is no Commandment greater than these."

"Well said, Teacher," the man replied. "You are right in saying that God is one and there is no other but him. To love him with all your heart, with all your understanding and with all your strength, and to love your neighbor as yourself is more important than all burnt offerings and sacrifices."

When Jesus saw that he had answered wisely, he said to him, "You are not far from the kingdom of God."
— Mark 12:28-34a

The most important Commandment of all is to love God more than anything else and love our neighbors as we love ourselves.

Some call Jesus' words the "Eleventh" Commandment. This command is originally found in Deuteronomy 6:4-9. In the New Testament, Jesus calls it the greatest, the first, and the most important Commandment. Jesus' words about this Commandment are found in Matthew 22, Luke 10, and Mark 12. Each has a unique twist.

In Matthew 22:34-40, the context for Jesus giving the greatest Commandment was a test by the Sadducees. They were trying to trap Jesus with a trick question, "Teacher, which is the greatest Commandment in the Law?" Jesus told them to love the Lord God first and foremost and the neighbor as self. "All the Law and the Prophets hang on these two Commandments," he said.

In Luke 10:25-28, the context of the greatest Commandment is an expert in the law trying to trick Jesus by asking him "What must I do to inherit eternal life?" Jesus replies, "What is written in the Law?" When the lawyer hears Jesus' question, he quotes Deuteronomy 6:4-5 about loving the Lord your God with heart, soul, strength, and mind and your neighbor as self. Jesus tells him that he is correct and that he should live what he believes. Then the lawyer, wanting to justify himself asks Jesus, "Who is my neighbor?"

Jesus then tells him the parable of the Good Samaritan, the point of which is not only to define our neighbor as one in need, but more to the point, to act like a good neighbor to the needy. We are called to act on our beliefs, not just express faith in intellectual terms. "Who is neighbor to the man who fell into the hands of robbers?" Jesus asks. "The one who had mercy on him," the lawyer responds. "Go and do likewise," Jesus says.

Whereas the context of the Eleventh Commandment in Matthew is the opportunity to summarize the Law and the Prophets against an opponent who is trying to trick him, the context in Luke is to be sure that an opponent doesn't just quote scripture, but acts on his faith.

In Mark, there is another twist in the context of the giving of the Eleventh Commandment. In Mark's Gospel, Jesus is dealing with a genuinely good man who wants to learn more from the astute teacher. The man, himself a teacher, is impressed by the debating skills of Jesus. He asks the question about the greatest of all Commandments because he really wants to know the proper priorities in life. Jesus tells him to love God more than anything else and love his neighbors as himself. When the man agrees with Jesus, he hears these words: "You aren't far from the kingdom of God." In Mark, the Eleventh Commandment is all about invitations to a new life.

Before we look at these invitations, let's examine the prohibitions, both stated and implied, in Matthew and Luke.

Prohibitions

The first prohibition in Matthew and Luke is that you can't win when you try to test God. In both of these gospels, an antagonist tries to trap Jesus by asking him about the greatest Commandment. In both cases, the antagonists are trapped in the trap they set for Jesus. Notice who wins the verbal "fist-a-cuffs" in both gospels.

The second prohibition is in all three synoptic gospel accounts. Jesus prohibits love of anything or anyone more than God. In the best sense, loving God is not a command, but the natural response to God's love for us, especially in the life, death, and resurrection of Jesus. God loves us; therefore we love God back. 1 John 4:7-10 puts it this way:

> *Dear friends, let us love one another, for love comes from God. Everyone who loves has been born of God and knows God. Whoever does not love does not know God, because* God is love. *This is how God showed his love among us; He sent his one and only Son into the world that we might live through him. This is love: not that we loved God, but that he loved us and sent his Son as an atoning sacrifice for our sins.*

The third prohibition in the Eleventh Commandment is that we can't love God and forget about our neighbor. The Eleventh Commandment is that since God loved us, we are called to love him back *and love our neighbors.* 1 John 4:11-12 puts it this way:

Dear friends, since God so loved us, we also ought to love one another. No one has ever seen God; but if we love one another, God lives in us and his love is made complete in us.

1 John 4:16 explains the reason to return the love of God. Verses 19-21 give us a practical example of faith active in love.

God is love ... We love because he first loved us. If anyone says, "I love God," yet hates his brother, he is a liar. For anyone who does not love his brother, whom he has seen, cannot love God, whom he has not seen. And he has given us this command: Whoever loves God must also love his brother.

In other words, the Eleventh Commandment prohibits just talking about love. We are invited to walk our talk and experience new life.

Invitations

First, to walk our talk about love means to accept Jesus' invitation to apply our faith to life by loving those who do not love us back. In other words, we are invited to take seriously the words of Jesus about loving our enemies.

Jesus put it this way in Matthew 5:43-48:

You have heard that it was said, "Love your neighbor and hate your enemy." But I tell you: Love your enemies and pray for those who persecute you, that you may be sons of your Father in heaven. He causes his sun to rise on the evil and the good, and sends rain on the righteous and unrighteous. If you love those who love you, what reward will you get? Are not even the tax collectors doing that? And if you greet only your brothers, what are you doing more than others? Do not even pagans do that? Be perfect, therefore, as your heavenly Father is perfect.

"Perfect" in Greek means "whole" or "complete," like God.

To love our enemies means to be like God. It does not mean that we have to like our enemies or approve of what they do. It means taking the initiative and acting toward people the way that God acts. He hates sins, but he loves the sinner. "Do not be overcome by evil, but overcome evil with good" (Romans 12:21). In other words, through Christ we can be proactive instead of reactive to those who do evil things against us.

Winston Churchill said, "Some people watch things happen. They are the professional critics. Some people don't know things happen. They are the sleepers. And some people make things happen. They are achievers and initiators." To love our enemies means by the power of God to be initiators in the area of human relations.

Second, to walk our talk about love means to accept Jesus' invitation to a new life. Natural man (and woman) pays back evil for evil. Natural man (and woman) wants to get even with those who cause hurt. Natural man (and woman) follows the lower part of human nature by getting trapped in the endless turmoil of reciprocity. Natural man (and woman) loves himself (herself) and puts down his (her) neighbor. Jesus invites us to a new way of life by loving God with our whole beings and loving our neighbors as we love ourselves.

On the streets of our cities we often see signs reading, "No U-turns." In the area of our relationship with God and one another, however, there is another sign: "God Allows U-turns." God even invites us to make U-turns and enter the new life. "I came to give life and give it in abundance," Jesus said.

How do we live this new life? By faith, worship, and works of love.

Faith in Jesus Christ as Lord and Savior brings new life. We don't achieve this faith; we receive it by the power of the Holy Spirit. Our part is to quit resisting what the Holy Spirit is doing to bring us to saving faith. Faith in Jesus Christ is trusting the one who died for us on the cross saying, "I'd rather die than give you up." Faith is loving God back for what he has done for us through Christ.

The new life includes faith. It also includes love for God through worship. To love the Lord means to worship him with all of our hearts and souls and minds and strength. In other words, to worship means to lose yourself in the act of adoration of the almighty. Worship means becoming transparent and getting caught up in the holy.

The new life means faith and worship. It also means faith active in love. Entering into works of love is not a matter of trying to earn salvation. We can't do that. Works of love toward our neighbors are expressions of gratitude for the love of God we have received through Jesus Christ.

To love our neighbors as ourselves means to speak and act like Jesus did. He spoke words of love to people who least expected it. He offered forgiveness to a woman caught in the act of adultery; to Matthew, a cheating tax collector; and to Peter who put his foot in his mouth so often than he had "foot-in-mouth disease." Jesus also asked forgiveness for those who were crucifying him. To offer forgiveness does not mean that the other person is forgiven. For the other person to be forgiven he or she must repent. We can't do that for someone else.

To offer forgiveness doesn't mean changing the person who hurts us; it means that we do what we can do. We change our attitude about those who are acting in evil ways. We cannot change other people. We can only change ourselves. To offer forgiveness means to take the initiative against evil by being willing to forgive.

"Yes," someone is saying, "but I'm not perfect." When people use the word "perfect," they usually mean, "without error." That's not what Jesus has in mind by saying, "You must be perfect as your Father in heaven is perfect." The word "perfect" in the English translation comes from the Greek word *teleos*. *Teleos* means whole, together, at peace. In other words, Jesus' words about being perfect are an invitation to have faith and be cleansed of the divisive elements in our nature and life. We are invited to be whole and together through forgiveness and at peace with God through trust in Jesus Christ as Lord and Savior.

Let me say that in a different way. The only way to love our enemies is to be like God in our loving.

"Dear friends, since God so loved us, we also ought to love one another" (1 John 4:11).

Questions For Your Personal Consideration And/Or Group Discussion

1. Read Deuteronomy 6:4-9. This creed of Israel is a summary of the Ten Commandments. It is called the *Shema*. Why were the Jews commanded to bind these words to their foreheads, their wrists, and their doors?

2. Read Matthew 22:34-40. The context here is _____ _____.

3. Read Luke 10:25-37. The context here is _____ _____.

4. Read Mark 12:28-34. The context here is _____ _____.

5. Consider these Prohibitions
   a. We can't get by with testing God (Matthew and Luke). We get trapped in our traps.
   b. We shouldn't love anything more than God.
   c. We can't love God and refuse to love our neighbor. See 1 John 4:11-12 and 1 John 4:19-21.

6. Consider these Invitations To Walk Our Talk.
   a. To love our enemies as well as our friends and family. See Matthew 5:43-48. The English word "perfect" here comes from the Greek word *teleos* which means whole or together, not without error. Romans 12:21 says "Do not be overcome by evil, but overcome evil with good." In other words, be proactive, not reactive with enemies.

   b. To accept Jesus' invitation to a new way to live. God allows U-turns.
      1. Faith
      2. Worship
      3. Works of love

Digging Deeper

1. The "Eleventh" or greatest Commandment calls us to love God back since he has loved us. In both John 3:16 and 1 Corinthians 13, the Greek word used to describe God's love for us is *agape*. This kind of love is not deserved; it is a gift. This kind of love is not achieved; it is received. This kind of love is not earned; it is an expression of God's grace.

2. Grace means God's loving action toward us in Jesus Christ. Justice means getting what we deserve. Mercy means not getting what we deserve. *Grace means getting what we do not deserve.*

3. Ephesians 4:32 says, "... be kind to one another." That sounds simple enough, but when you consider the Greek word *chestos* we so easily translate "kind," another meaning surfaces. *Chestos* means more than being nice to people. It means doing what God does. "... he [God] is kind to the unthankful and to the sinners" (Luke 6:36). The admonition "be kind to one another" is not a pious platitude, but an invitation to put the "Eleventh" Commandment into action by doing what God does.

4. To love God and neighbor is a major uphill battle today. You've got to fight to do right in a secular culture that urges, "Me first, last, and always."

5. The late Steve Allen deplored what he called "the tidal wave of barbaric ugliness, both moral and aesthetic, that now dominates the American culture." In his book *Vulgarians At the Gate*, Allen says, "The coarsening of our entire culture is by no means a simple matter. But oppose it we must ... (because the) social atmosphere characterized by vulgarity, violence, brutish manners, the collapse of the family, and general disrespect for traditional codes of conduct is to chill the blood of even the most tolerant observers."

6. In spite of what is happening all around us, there is hope that transformation can happen to us and others we love because there is a magnetic attraction in the new affection called *agape* (love). Once you've experienced it from God through Christ, you want to pass it on.

Chapter Twelve
Life Begins At Forty

The context for God giving the Ten Commandments to the Hebrews is their *forty* year journey in the wilderness. Actually, it only took them about one year to travel from Egypt to the promised land, but then because of disobedience, they wandered in the wilderness for a total of forty years. The number *forty* fascinates me.

First, let's look back in the Old Testament before the time of the exodus and discover the number *forty* in Hebrew history, as described by Stephen, the first Christian martyr, in the seventh chapter of Acts.

When he was *forty* years old, Moses, the Egyptian Prince, visited his relatives, the Hebrews (Acts 7:23 NRSV). When he saw that one of his fellow Hebrews was being mistreated, Moses defended the oppressed man and struck down and killed the Egyptian guard. Frightened, Moses fled from Egypt and went to the land of Midian, at the foot of Mount Sinai. How long did Moses stay in Midian?

We pick up the story as Stephen told it:

> *Now when forty years had passed, an angel appeared to him in the wilderness of Mount Sinai, in the flame of a burning bush. When Moses saw it, he was amazed at the sight; and as he approached to look, there came the voice of the Lord: "I am the God of your ancestors, the God of Abraham, Isaac, and Jacob."* Moses

> *began to tremble and did not dare to look. Then the Lord said to him,*
>
> *"Take off the sandals from your feet, for the place where you are standing is holy ground. I have surely seen the mistreatment of my people who are in Egypt and have heard their groaning, and I have come down to rescue them. Come now, I will send you to Egypt."*
>
> — Acts 7:30-34 (NRSV)

Stephen then describes the *forty* years the Hebrews wandered in the wilderness with Moses as the servant of the God who liberated people by performing wonders, signs, and miracles (Acts 7:35-36). In just thirteen verses, Stephen mentions *forty* as a significant number three times. What does *forty* mean?

According to Exodus, how long was Moses, the pre-figure of Christ, on Mount Sinai receiving the Ten Commandments from God? Wasn't it *forty* days? Why does the Old Testament use this number *forty* as if it has special meaning? Is it a coded telegram? What significance does *forty* have? Good question.

Second, if we go forward in history to the New Testament, don't we discover that Jesus fasted in the wilderness for (you guessed it) *forty* days? Why *forty*? Why not thirty-nine or forty-one? What does this number *forty* signify? What is the Bible trying to tell us by the repeated use of *forty*?

Maybe *forty* stands for readiness to do mighty deeds for the mighty God in a new chapter of life. A *forty*-year-old Moses was ready to start a new chapter of his life by going to Midian where in *forty* years God got him ready to become a mighty leader. The Hebrews were molded into the people of God in their *forty* years in the wilderness. They were getting ready to enter a new chapter in their lives by entering the promised land. In the *forty* days on Mount Sinai, Moses was getting ready to lead the Hebrews into a new chapter of their lives under the dominion of God and his Laws.

In the wilderness temptations, Jesus was getting ready to serve God by his mighty deeds and wonders as well as by his quiet teachings and his unparalleled suffering and sacrificial death. After the temptations in the wilderness, wasn't it starting-again-time for Jesus who invited people to start their lives again under God?

Didn't the people of old figure that living until *forty* was living a lifetime? If so, when you go beyond *forty*, aren't you starting a new life?

Could *forty* be one of those biblical numbers with great symbolic meaning, like *one* (God's unity), *three* (the Trinity), *four* (the four "corners" of the universe or the four directions — north, east, south and west), *seven* (the seven days of the week, the perfect number, meaning wholeness), *twelve* (the twelve tribes of Israel and the twelve apostles) and *ten* (the perfect Law of God)?

Symbolically, could *forty* be *ten* (the perfect Law of God) times *four* (all directions we can go), meaning that wherever we go, the Law of God rules supreme? Just speculation of course, and yet,

if you do the math ...

10 the BIG TEN, that is
x 4 north, east, south, and west
40 an invitation to start your life again under the reign of God's Commandments and love

Didn't someone say,

"Life begins at forty"?

Seven Tips For Leaders

Below find seven tips for pastors who use this material for instruction classes for new members, for teachers of confirmation classes, Sunday school classes for adults and teenagers, and for leaders of small groups. The small groups may meet in the homes of participants or at the church.

1. Start and/or end each study with prayer.

2. For best results, all participants should have copies of *The Big Ten*. However, the book is designed so that the leader or teacher can use it as a study guide and participants can use their Bibles without a copy of the book. If you choose the latter method, it is cheaper, but not better. At the very least, copies of *The Big Ten* should be made available for all participants who want them.

3. Use the questions at the end of each chapter as group discussion starters or for personal reflection.

4. As time allows, use Digging Deeper at the end of each chapter for further background, insight, and application.

5. *The Big Ten* is designed to be used weekly, bi-monthly, or monthly by groups or classes. The book may be used for twelve study sessions. If twelve sessions are not possible for your group, the study can be done in five, six, or eight sessions by combining chapters.

6. Rather than lecturing on the topics, try to get members of your class or group involved in discussion of the topics in the chapters. Participation results in increased understanding and retention.

7. One of the ways to get people involved in participation in your class or group is to use small group techniques. Many small group techniques and information on starting small groups and keeping them going are found in *Way To Grow! Dynamic Church Growth Through Small Groups* by Ron Lavin, CSS Publishing Company, Lima, Ohio, 1996. This book and others by Ron Lavin may be ordered by using the information below:

CSS Publishing Company
517 South Main Street
P.O. Box 4503
Lima, Ohio 45802-4503

1-800-537-1030

e-mail: orders@csspub.com

fax: 1-419-228-9184

Endnotes

Foundations
1. Ron Lavin, *I Believe; Help My Unbelief: Another Look At The Apostles' Creed* (Lima, Ohio: CSS Publishing Company, Inc., 2002).

Chapter 1
2. Martin Luther, *The Small Catechism* (Minneapolis, Minnesota: Augsburg Publishing House, 1979), p. 3.

3. Robert Tuttle, *The Runway* (Lima, Ohio: CSS Publishing Company, Inc., 1997).

Chapter 2
4. Luther, *op. cit.*, p. 3.

5. John Davis and Henry Snyder Gehman, *The Westminster Dictionary Of The Bible* (Philadelphia: The Westminster Press, 1944), p. 418.

6. *Ibid.*, p. 206.

7. *Ibid.*, p. 206.

Chapter 3
8. Luther, *op. cit.*, p. 4.

9. Henri Nouwen, *The Living Reminder* (New York: Seabury Press, 1977), p. 38.

10. For further exposition on Psalm 73 and other Psalms, see *Turning Griping Into Gratitude* (Lima, Ohio: CSS Publishing Company, Inc., 2000).

Chapter 6
11. Willard F. Harley, Jr., *His Needs, Her Needs: Building An Affair Proof Marriage* (Old Tappan, New Jersey: Fleming H. Revell Publishers, 1986), pp. 12-13.

12. Gary and Barbara Rosberg, *The Five Love Needs Of Men And Women*, Wheaton, Illinois: Tyndale, 2000).

Chapter 8
13. Luther, *op. cit.*, p. 6.

Chapter 10
14. Ron Lavin, *op. cit.*, *Turning Griping Into Gratitude*.

www.ingramcontent.com/pod-product-compliance
Lightning Source LLC
Chambersburg PA
CBHW071723090426
42738CB00009B/1854